GLENORCHY

INTRO

Neuseeland hat auf unserer Landkarte aller bewohnten und befahrbaren Welten eine Art Wild Card: zu weit weg, um zu den naheliegenden Superstars einer Reise-Bucketlist zu gehören, irgendwie aber auch den unruhigen Herzen aller Reise-Fanatiker so nahe, dass wir uns unbedingt eine Start-Erlaubnis zum großen Neuseeland-Abenteuer geben mussten. Vielleicht liegt der Reiz des Landes zwischen Australien und Antarktis aus der Ferne ja auch einfach nur an seiner Lage am Rand der schier endlosen Weite des Südpazifiks. Hier hört wirklich die Welt auf. Hier ist der Tag schon zu Ende, wenn er an anderen Orten der Welt gerade beginnt. Zugegeben – allein das mag Menschen mit Reise-Virus unwiderstehlich anziehen: „Lass uns so weit fahren, wie nur irgend möglich." Natürlich können wir uns diesem Sog des unersättlichen Fernwehs nicht entziehen, er ist aber nicht der Stoff, aus dem CURVES gewoben wird. CURVES – das ist die Suche nach dem Moment. Nach einer Schönheit, die im Hier und Jetzt gefunden wird. Das Eintauchen in den Flow. Und all das haben wir auf Neuseeland entdeckt: übergroße Momente für Heldensagen und feinsinnige Momente von sanfter Schönheit. Unterwegssein in unbeschreiblicher Schönheit und dichter Monotonie. Schweigendes Fahren nach innen hinein und leidenschaftliches Fahren ins Weite hinaus. Wir nennen das: *Soulful Driving*. Kommen Sie mit nach Neuseeland. Entdecken Sie Aotearoa, das Land der langen, weißen Wolke, mit CURVES.

—

New Zealand occupies a kind of wild card status on our map of all inhabited and navigable worlds: too far away to be one of the obvious superstars on a travel bucket list, but somehow also so close to the restless hearts of all travel fanatics that we definitely have to green-light a big New Zealand adventure. When viewed from a distance, it is possible that the charm of these islands between Australia and Antarctica simply lies in their location on the edge of the seemingly endless expanse of the South Pacific. The world really does end here. Here the day is already over when it is just beginning in other places in the world. Admittedly, that fact alone may make it irresistibly attractive to people with the travel bug: "Let's drive as far as we possibly can." Naturally, we cannot escape the insatiable draw of this wanderlust, but that's not really what CURVES is all about. CURVES embodies a search for the moment and the beauty that is found in the here and now. It's all about immersing yourself in the flow. We discovered all of this in New Zealand: gigantic moments drawn from heroic sagas and subtle moments of gentle beauty. Our travels brought us experiences of indescribable beauty and dense monotony. Moments of silent introspection were followed by periods of passionate exuberance. This is what we call *soulful driving*. Join us in New Zealand. Discover Aotearoa, the land of the long white cloud, with CURVES.

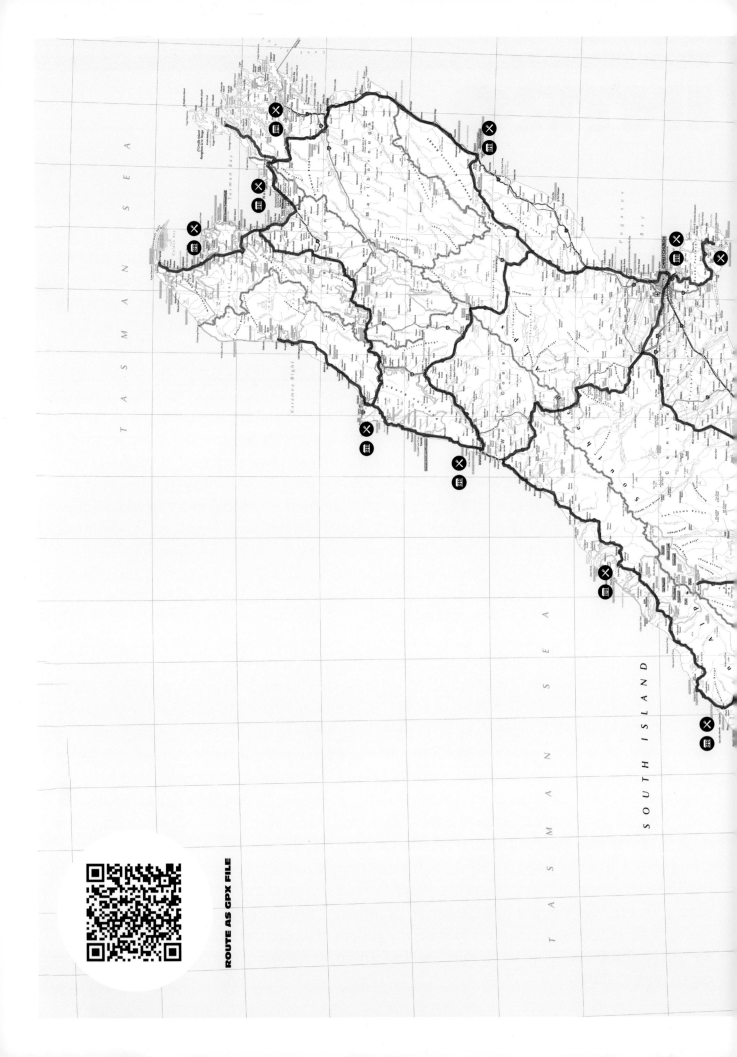

ROUTE AS GPX FILE

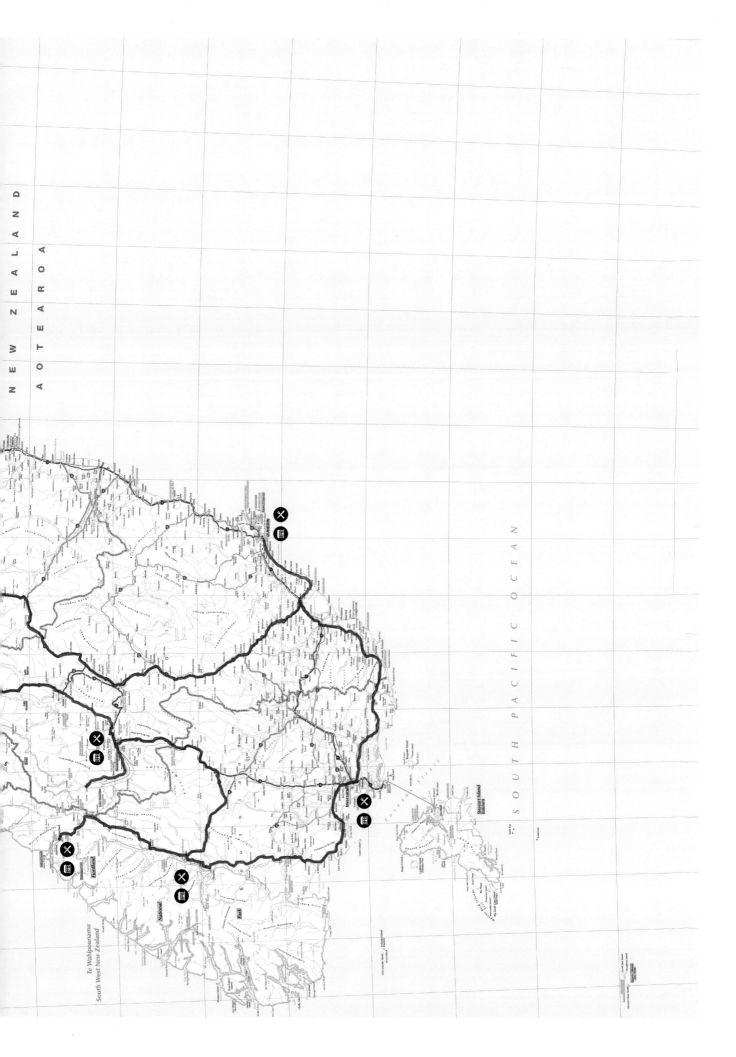

MOUNT COOK ROAD

1
ETAPPE
STAGE

2
ETAPPE
STAGE

Unsere Reise über die Südinsel Neuseelands beginnt in Christchurch. Die größte Stadt des Südens liegt an der Ostküste, durch eine vorgelagerte Halbinsel gut geschützt vor dem rauen Pazifik. Die Kilometer in der flachen Küstenebene nutzen wir für ein erstes Zurechtfinden: ungewohnter Linksverkehr, der Kulturmix aus angelsächsischen Standards und neuseeländischen Spezialitäten, die bemerkenswerte Freundlichkeit der Menschen. Dass die ganze Zeit die Berge der neuseeländischen Alpen im Westen mit uns ziehen, erhöht unsere Vorfreude auf kommende Etappen und würzt die eher reizarme Streckenführung immer wieder. Bei Blenheim haben wir die Berge des Nordens erreicht, hier ist der Lauf des Wairau-Flusses eine scharfe Grenze zwischen Schwemmebenen und bis zu 1.000 Meter hohen Bergen, die eine wild zerfaserte Küste aus Inseln, Schären und Fjorden bilden. Den Abstecher zum „French Pass" – einer gefährlichen Meerenge zwischen Festland und Insel – wollen wir uns nicht entgehen lassen, er sorgt zum ersten Mal andauernd und intensiv für echte CURVES-Schwingungen. Gut warmgefahren geht es dann zum Cape Farewell, einer langen Landzunge am äußersten Zipfel der Südinsel.

Von ganz im Norden, bis in den westlichsten Westen, über die Berge und zurück an den Anfang: Das ist eine ganz grobe Kurzfassung der zweiten Etappe über die Südinsel Neuseelands. Wir beginnen am Cape Farewell mit seinen mächtigen Steilklippen und der sich viele Kilometer weit nach Osten krümmenden Landzunge, fahren danach in weitem Bogen rund um den Kahurangi Nationalpark und treffen am Cape Foulwind wieder auf die Westküste. Die zweite Hälfte der Etappe ist dann weniger vom Meer geprägt, sondern vom gebirgigen Landesinneren. Über das Tal des Grey River fahren wir in die Gold- und Kohlestadt Reefton, von hier aus geht es über den Rahu Saddle, Springs Junction und den Lewis Pass über den Hauptkamm der neuseeländischen Alpen. Die zeigen hier oben noch einen eher milden Charakter und ergießen viele gerölltragende Ströme nach Osten zum Pazifik. Diesen Flüssen folgen wir, drehen dann nach Süden ab und fahren zurück bis Christchurch. Das Ende der Etappe krönen wir dann mit einer Runde durch die Berge der Banks-Halbinsel, die eine Art Mini-Neuseeland an sich darstellen: Berge und Meer, Vielseitigkeit und Schönheit.

Our journey across New Zealand's South Island begins in Christchurch. The largest city in the south, it is located on the east coast, well protected from the rough Pacific by an offshore peninsula. The flat coastal plain affords us an opportunity to come to terms with our surroundings: unusual left-hand traffic, the cultural mix of standard Anglo-Saxon sights and New Zealand exoticism, the remarkable friendliness of the people. The fact that the mountains of the New Zealand Alps to the west follow us on our journey increases our anticipation for the coming stages and spices up what is otherwise a rather unexciting section. At Blenheim we have reached the mountains of the north, where the course of the Wairau River forms a sharp boundary between flood plains and mountains up to 1,000 meters high in a wildly fragmented coastline of islands, skerries and fjords. We are anxious not to miss the detour to the "French Pass" – a dangerous strait between the mainland and the island - because this is the first chance to experience the continuously intense conditions you've come to expect from CURVES. Thoroughly warmed up, we head for Cape Farewell, a long headland at the very tip of the South Island.

From the far north, to the most westerly parts, over the mountains and back to the beginning: this is a very rough summary of the second stage across the South Island of New Zealand. We start at Cape Farewell with its mighty cliffs and the headland that curves for many kilometers to the east, then drive in a wide arc around the Kahurangi National Park, meeting the west coast again at Cape Foulwind. The second half of the stage is characterized less by the sea and more by the mountainous interior. We drive across the Gray River valley to the gold and coal mining town of Reefton. From here we move over the Rahu Saddle, Springs Junction and the Lewis Pass to cross the main ridge of the New Zealand Alps. Up here the mountains still seem fairly mild and benign, with many boulder-bearing streams eastwards to the Pacific. We follow these rivers, then turn south and drive back to Christchurch. We then crown the final part of the stage with a lap of the mountains of the Banks Peninsula, which are like New Zealand in miniature: mountains and sea, diversity and beauty.

3

4

Auch auf der dritten Etappe überqueren wir die Südinsel Neuseelands und die Bergkette der neuseeländischen Alpen einmal komplett, von Ost nach West. Mit einer Fahrt über die bildschöne Banks-Halbinsel fahren wir uns zuerst warm und machen uns dann auf den langen Weg durch die Ebene des Waimakariri-Flusses nach Westen. Über den Porters Pass und Castle Hill dringen wir ins Innere des Gebirges vor, treffen am Arthurs Pass erneut auf den Waimakariri und fahren dann am Fuß des Mount Temple zur Westseite der Alpen. Mit dem Flusstal des Taramakau gelangen wir zum Pazifik und haben nun viele Kilometer am Meer vor uns. Ausgebremst wird die Route an der Küste entlang immer wieder durch große Flüsse, die in ausladenden Betten große Mengen Geröll aus den Bergen heruntertragen: Der Mikonui, der Waitaha, der Wanganui, der Poerua und schließlich der Whataroa. Es folgen die Schmelzwasserabflüsse des Franz-Josef-Gletschers und des Fox-Gletschers – bei Haast verlassen wir diese wilde Küste endgültig. Über den River Haast geht es nun in die Berge hinein, bis zu den Trogtälern des Lake Wānaka, und Lake Hawea. Und hier haben wir nun das im Süden anschließende Cardrona Valley sowie die Crown Range am Übergang in Richtung Queenstown erreicht.

___

On the third stage we once again cross the South Island of New Zealand and the mountain range of the New Zealand Alps completely, moving from east to west. We advance into the interior of the mountains via Porters Pass and Castle Hill, encountering the Waimakariri again at Arthurs Pass and then driving to the western side of the Alps in the shadow of Mount Temple. The Taramakau river valley ushers us to the Pacific and we now have many kilometers of coastline ahead of us. The route along the coast is repeatedly interrupted by major rivers that carry large amounts of rubble down from the mountains in broad beds: the Mikonui, the Waitaha, the Wanganui, the Poerua and finally the Whataroa. We then come upon the meltwater outflows of the Franz Josef Glacier and the Fox Glacier. We finally leave this wild coast at Haast. Crossing the River Haast, we now enter the mountains, driving as far as the trough-like valleys of Lake Wānaka and Lake Hawea. We have now reached the Cardrona Valley in the south and the Crown Range as we swing towards Queenstown.

Die Fjord-artigen Seen Wakatipu und Te Anau prägen die erste Hälfte dieser Etappe. Im Norden des Lake Wakatipu kommen Fans der „Herr der Ringe"-Verfilmung auf ihre Kosten: Der von Glenorchy aus zu sehende Mount Earnslaw eröffnet „Die zwei Türme", das reale Landschaftsdouble des Film-Elbenreichs Lothlórien findet sich ebenfalls hier oben. Aber auch im Süden geht das Fest für Film-Fans weiter, der Waiau River zwischen Te Anau und Manapouri wurde von Regisseur Peter Jackson im Film zum „Anduin" erklärt, die Wälder an der Takaro Road hinter Te Anau zum „Fangorn"-Wald aus dem Fantasy-Epos. Natürlich müssen aber auch Reisende, die keine Fan-Beziehung zu Buch oder Film aufgebaut haben, nicht auf cineastische Momente verzichten. Die vielseitigen Landschaften der neuseeländischen Südinsel sind so spektakulär, dass man sich keine Hobbits, Orks und Elben in sie hinein vorzustellen braucht, um immer wieder von ihrer Schönheit berührt zu werden. Ein erster Höhepunkt ist der Besuch des Milford Sound – einem vom Pazifik über 15 Kilometer ins Landesinnere hineinragenden Fjord. In seinen Gewässern leben Delfine, Seehunde und Zwergpinguine, unter den Berg-Charakterdarstellern an seinen Ufern ist besonders der steil aufragende Mitre Peak zu nennen. Von hier aus führt die Route dann hinunter an die südlichste Küste Neuseelands, bei Invercargill.

___

The fjord-like lakes Wakatipu and Te Anau dominate the first half of this stage. In the north of Lake Wakatipu, fans of the "Lord of the Rings" film series will be in seventh heaven: Mount Earnslaw, which can be seen from Glenorchy, provides the opening shots for "The Two Towers", and the real landscape double of the elven kingdom of Lothlórien can also be found up here. However the treat for film fans also continues in the south, the Waiau River between Te Anau and Manapouri was used as the "Anduin" by director Peter Jackson, while the forests on Takaro Road behind Te Anau served as the "Fangorn" forest from the fantasy epic. Of course, even travelers who are not (yet) fans of the books or movies can still enjoy the cinematic moments. The diverse landscapes of New Zealand's South Island are so spectacular that you don't need to imagine hobbits, orcs and elves in them to be constantly touched by their beauty. A first highlight is a visit to Milford Sound – a fjord that extends over 15 kilometers inland from the Pacific. Dolphins, seals and dwarf penguins live in its waters, and the steep Miter Peak is particularly notable among the mountains on its banks. From here the route leads down to the southernmost coast of New Zealand, near Invercargill.

5

ETAPPE
STAGE

LINDIS PASS

Invercargill ist mit ihren rund 55.000 Einwohnern die südlichste Großstadt Neuseelands, hier starten wir in die letzte Etappe unserer Reise. Übrigens: Der südlichste Punkt Neuseelands liegt auf den rund 600 Kilometer entfernt im subantarktischen Ozean liegenden, unbewohnten Campbell-Inseln. Die Etappe hinter Invercargill beginnt mit vielen Kilometern in landwirtschaftlich geprägten Gegenden, groovt sich dann auf den Küstenstraßen südlich des Catlins National Forest ins Reisetempo ein und kurvt dann über Balclutha und Milton bis nach Dunedin. Die dort liegende Otago-Halbinsel ist diesen Abstecher auf jeden Fall wert. Zurück in Milton setzen wir die Fahrt in Richtung Nordwesten fort, gelangen im Landesinneren so bis Alexandra und fahren von hier in nördlicher Richtung bis zum Lake Pukaki. Der Pukaki-See ist ein Schmelzwasser-See der ehemaligen Gebirgsgletscher, an seinem Nordende thronen die schnee- und eisbedeckten Gipfel des Aoraki-/Mount-Cook-Massivs, die auch heute noch dicke Gletscherkappen bewahren. Wieder fahren wir den Weg zurück nach Süden, setzen dann die Reise am Südende des Sees weiter nach Osten, streifen den Lake Tekapo und rollen nun in Richtung Osten. Nach vielen Kilometern aus dem Gebirge hinaus und dann der Fahrt durch die vorgelagerte Küstenebene, sind wir wieder in Christchurch angelangt.

With a population of around 55,000, Invercargill is the southernmost city in New Zealand. This is where we start the last leg of our journey. The first part of the stage beyond Invercargill consists of many kilometers of agricultural land, after which we groove at cruising pace along the coastal roads south of the Catlins National Forest and then curve through Balclutha and Milton to Dunedin. The Otago Peninsula is definitely worth this detour. Back in Milton we continue our journey north-west, reaching Alexandra inland and from there driving north to Lake Pukaki. Lake Pukaki is a meltwater lake created by the former mountain glaciers; at its northern end are the snow- and ice-covered peaks of the Aoraki/Mount Cook massif, which still retain thick glacial caps today. We drive back south, then continue the journey east at the southern end of the lake, touch Lake Tekapo and now head east. After many kilometers we emerge from the mountains and then, after driving through the coastal plain, we arrive back in Christchurch.

EDITORIAL

Drei. Sieben. Acht. Zwölf. Vierzig. Solche Zahlen tauchen immer dann auf, wenn Menschen etwas erzählen wollen, das über sie hinausreicht. Über die Zeit hinaus, über das Individuum hinaus. Diese Zahlen sind nicht real – sie sind hyperreal. Geschichten, in denen Dinge dreifach, achtfach, vierzigfach vorkommen, sind also nicht wahr, aber sie erzählen etwas Substanzielles. Etwas Größeres als die Wahrheit. Vierzig Kanus machen der Überlieferung nach die „Große Flotte" der Maori-Vorfahren aus, die irgendwann zwischen 1280 und 1350 über den Pazifik fuhr, um aus Polynesien kommend Neuseeland zu besiedeln. Andere Geschichten sagen, es seien sieben Kanus gewesen und wenn man die Stämme der Maori fragt, führen sie sich auf die Insassen von acht Kanus zurück. So oder so, ob sieben, acht oder vierzig Kanus – die eigentliche Geschichte geht so: Wir sind hier, dies ist unser Anfang, dieses Land gehört uns. Die weit hinten über den Wasserwüsten des Pazifik liegende, mythische Vergangenheit wird damit zum Bedeutungsverstärker. Und die Fahrt der Kanus ins Land der großen weißen Wolke, „Aotearoa", zur Geburtsstunde der Maori.

Die Erinnerungen der Maori reichen allerdings noch über 350 Jahre vor die Fahrt der Großen Flotte zurück: Ungefähr 925 n. Chr. soll ein mythischer Vorfahr namens Kupe auf weiten Streifzügen über den Pazifik Neuseeland entdeckt und das Wissen um die Existenz des Landes in seine Heimat zurückgetragen haben. Die heißt „Hawaiki", ist auf keiner Landkarte zu finden, bedeutet selbst in der Sprache der Maori nichts anderes als „Unterwelt" und ist damit eine Metapher für den Urgrund der Maori. Wieder so eine Hyperrealität, die für den Glauben der Polynesier bezeichnend ist: In einer Welt der extremen Elemente gehen Wirklichkeit und Jenseits ineinander über, sind eins. – Vielleicht hat sich alles ja ungefähr so zugetragen: 3.000 bis 2.500 Jahre vor unserer Zeitrechnung könnten Menschen aus der Gegend des heutigen Taiwan aufs Meer hinausgefahren sein. Zu den Inselwelten der Philippinen und Indonesiens, von dort über Generationen hinweg immer weiter in die immer wässrigere Weite des Pazifik hinein. Sie wurden zu den Bewohnern Polynesiens, besiedelten die Fiji-Inseln, Samoa, Tonga, Tahiti und die Cook-Inseln, fuhren bis hinauf nach Hawaii, hinüber zu den letzten Archipelen vor der leeren Weite des Pazifik, hinunter zu den Osterinseln. Und dann, während in Asien die Mongolen das größte Landreich der Weltgeschichte errichteten und

Three, seven, eight, twelve and forty are all magic numbers. They are always used when people want to tell about something unfathomable, beyond time, beyond the individual. These numbers are not real – they are hyperreal. Hence, stories in which things appear three times, eight times, forty times are not true, but they tell us something substantial, some greater truth. Tradition tells us that the "Great Fleet" of the Maori ancestors that sailed across the Pacific sometime between 1280 and 1350 to settle New Zealand from Polynesia consisted of forty canoes. Other versions of the tale say there were seven canoes and if you ask members of the Maori tribes themselves, they will attribute their origins to the occupants of eight canoes. Either way, whether seven, eight or forty canoes – the real story goes like this: we are here, this is our beginning, this land is ours. The mythical past, stretching far back over the watery expanses of the Pacific, lends greater meaning to the journey of the canoes to the land of the great white cloud, "Aotearoa" and the birth of the Maori people.

However, Maori memories go back even further: over 350 years before the voyage of the Great Fleet, in around 925 AD, a mythical ancestor named Kupe is said to have discovered New Zealand on long forays across the Pacific, bringing his knowledge of the country's existence back to his homeland. This was a place called "Hawaiki". It can't be found on any map, and even in the Maori language it simply means "underworld" and is therefore a metaphor for the origins of the Maori, another example of the hyperreality that is typical of the beliefs of the Polynesians; in a world of extreme elements, reality and the afterlife merge into one another and become one. It is possible that it all happened something like this: 3,000 to 2,500 years before our era, people from the area of today's Taiwan could have sailed out to sea, to the island worlds of the Philippines and Indonesia. From there, over generations they may have spread further and further into the wide blue yonder of the Pacific. They became the inhabitants of Polynesia, settled the Fiji Islands, Samoa, Tonga, Tahiti and the Cook Islands, sailing up as far as Hawaii, over to the last archipelagos before the empty expanse of the Pacific, then down to Easter Island. And then, while the Mongols were building the largest land empire in world history in Asia and Europe was sending Christian crusaders to the Middle East, the Polynesians were heading for New Zealand.

Europa christliche Kreuzfahrer in den Nahen Osten schickte, nahmen die Polynesier Kurs auf Neuseeland.

Die Insel war nur gegen die großen Windrichtungen zu erreichen, eine solche monatelange Fahrt unternimmt man nicht so leicht, selbst wenn man ein Mensch der Wasserwelten ist. Dass diese Fahrten überhaupt möglich waren, liegt an den Waka, den Kanus der Maori-Vorfahren. Man darf sie sich nicht klein und leicht und zerbrechlich vorstellen, sondern eher als zwischen sechs und dreißig Meter lange Einbäume, mit Platz für bis zu 100 Menschen und Körben voller Proviant und Saatgut, mit flexiblen Segeln und langen Auslegern. Vielleicht hat man sie auch in Paaren zu einer Art Katamaran verbunden, um so auf hoher See für mehr Stabilität zu sorgen. Und die Waka waren keine nüchternen technischen Geräte im europäischen Sinn, sondern schwimmende Wesenheiten mit geschnitzten Rümpfen, auf denen sich Seeungeheuer und Lebewesen des Meeres wanden, an deren Bug und Heck mythische Figuren geiferten. Man darf gern an Wikinger-Drachenboote denken, um den Spirit dieser Reisegefährten über den Ozean ansatzweise zu verstehen.

Am 13. Dezember 1642 wird Aotearoa, das Land der großen weißen Wolke, dann zum ersten Mal durch niederländische Seefahrer entdeckt. Zu Beginn glauben sie noch im viele tausend Kilometer weit entfernten Chile zu sein, ein Jahr später wird der Irrtum durch eine nachfolgende Expedition korrigiert. Die rund um den Globus nach Bodenschätzen und Handelschancen trüffelnden Niederländer verzeichnen damals das heutige New York als „Nieuw Amsterdam" in ihren Karten, Australien ist für sie „Nieuw Holland". Nun bekommt auch das Aotearoa der Maori einen europäischen Namen, die südlichste niederländische Provinz „Zeeland" wird zum Paten. Es ist aber eine Expedition um den britischen Kapitän James Cook, die „Nieuw Zeeland" als erste Europäer intensiver erforscht, es folgen französische Entdecker, dann Walfänger, Robbenfänger und schließlich Missionare, die den Maori christliche Werte beibringen sollen. Die Ureinwohner haben sich nach ersten gewalttätigen Verspannungen schnell an den Handel und das Zusammenleben mit den neuen Besuchern und Nachbarn vom anderen Ende der Welt gewöhnt, pflegen aber ihre traditionellen Stammesstrukturen weiter, zu denen regelrecht rituelle, jährliche Kriegszüge gegeneinander gehören. Es sind daher nicht die an-

The island could only be reached by sailing against the strong winds; it is not easy to undertake such a long journey, even if you are a seasoned sea-dog. The fact that these trips were possible at all is due to the waka, the canoes used the Maori ancestors. You shouldn't imagine them as small, light and fragile vessels, but rather as dugout canoes between six and thirty meters long, with space for up to 100 people and baskets full of provisions and seeds, with flexible sails and long outriggers. They may have been connected in pairs to form a kind of catamaran to ensure greater stability on the high seas. And the waka were not sober technical craft in the European sense, but water-borne beings with carved hulls depicting writhing sea monsters and other creatures and with mythical figures looming at the bow and stern. It is probably more accurate to compare the boats to Viking longships in order to get an inkling of the spirit of these ocean travelers.

Aotearoa, the land of the great white cloud, was first discovered for the first time by Dutch sailors on December 13, 1642. Initially, they thought they had landed in Chile, thousands of kilometers away, but a year later the mistake was corrected by a follow-up expedition. At that time, the Dutch, who were searching the globe for mineral resources and trade opportunities, referred to today's New York as "Nieuw Amsterdam" on their maps, while Australia was known to them as "Nieuw Holland". The Maori's Aotearoa was now also given a European name, with the southernmost Dutch province of "Zeeland" providing the patronym. However, it was an expedition led by the British captain James Cook that was the first European group to explore "Nieuw Zeeland" more intensively, followed by French explorers, then whalers, sealers and, finally, missionaries, who were determined to teach Christian values to the Maori. After initial violent tensions, the natives quickly got used to trading and living side-by-side with new visitors and neighbors from the other side of the world, but continued to maintain their traditional tribal structures, which included ritual, annual campaigns of war against one another. Thus, it was not the Europeans' contagious diseases or Christian attempts at colonization that posed the greatest threat to the Maori, but rather the weapons imported from Europe: at the beginning of the 1830s, various Maori tribes equipped themselves with European-made flintlock muskets and carried out outright massacres on each other over a period of five years.

steckenden Krankheiten der Europäer und nicht ihre christlichen Kolonialisierungsversuche, die zur größten Bedrohung der Maori werden, sondern die Waffen aus Europa: Zu Beginn der 1830er-Jahre versorgen sich verschiedene Maori-Stämme mit Steinschloss-Musketen aus europäischer Produktion und richten über fünf Jahre hinweg regelrechte Massaker untereinander an. Erst nach vielen tausenden Toten können die Exzesse mit einem Friedensvertrag gestoppt werden – und auch das vielleicht nur, weil ein steter Zufluss von Musketen inzwischen für Waffengleichheit gesorgt hat.

Das entstandene Gleichgewicht der nun „Vereinigten Stämme" kassieren die Briten, annektieren „New Zeeland" als Teil des britischen Weltreichs und üben von da an politische Kontrolle aus. Zuerst wird Neuseeland als britische Kolonie geführt, ab 1907 als Dominion – und auch heute noch ist der britische König Charles III. hierarchisches Staatsoberhaupt. Der Premierminister Neuseelands steht so gesehen hinter der die britische Krone vertretenden Generalgouverneurin erst an dritter Stelle.

Aber Neuseeland ist nicht nur durch seinen Aufstieg aus einem mythischen Nebel, als Sagen-Ziel seiner Ureinwohner und den nur wenige hundert Jahre währenden Parforce-Ritt des gesellschaftlichen Werdens eine absolute Besonderheit, sondern auch in seiner Geologie, seiner Evolution von Flora und Fauna. Die Inseln Neuseelands gehören für die meisten zu Australien, in Wahrheit sind sie ein Resultat des Zerfallens einer Ur-Erde: Vor Millionen von Jahren zerbirst Gondwana, die südliche Hälfte des Urkontinents Pangäea. Südamerika und Afrika schmiegen sich damals in Löffelchenstellung aneinander, in ihren Rücken legt sich eine durch das heutige Indien, Australien und Antarktika gebildete Landmasse. Dann treiben titanenhafte Kräfte im Erdinneren die Kruste auseinander: Südamerika verliert seinen Milliarden Jahre alten Kontakt zu Afrika und macht sich auf eine weite Reise nach Westen. Indien löst sich vom afrikanischen Süden, lässt dabei einen Fetzen zurück, den man heute Madagaskar nennt, segelt in einem Hunderttausende-Jahre-Zeitraffer energisch nach Norden davon und rumst dort so brachial in die zögerlich umherdümpelnde Landmasse Asiens, dass beim Crash der nahezu neun Kilometer hohe Himalaya aufgeknittert wird. Im Süden kurven derweil Antarktika und Australien im Engtanz dahin, können zuerst nicht so recht voneinander lassen, aber dann entscheidet sich Antarktika doch für eine eiskalte Zukunft am Südpol und Australien verzieht sich beleidigt mit Kurs Nordost. Die Antarktis hat es nun

Many thousands died before these excesses were halted with a peace treaty – and even then perhaps only because a constant supply of muskets ensured equality of arms.

The British made the most of the resulting balance between the now "United Tribes" and annexed "New Zeeland" as part of the British Empire and from then on exercised political control. New Zealand was initially run as a British colony, then as a dominion from 1907. It is still ruled by the British King Charles III today as hierarchical head of state. Thus, strictly speaking, the Prime Minister of New Zealand only takes third place in the pecking order, behind the Governor General, who represents the British Crown.

However, New Zealand is quite unique not only for its rise from the mists of seafaring tales, as the legendary destination of its native people and the tour de force of social development that took just a few hundred years, but also for its geology and its evolution of flora and fauna. In geographical terms, most people regard the islands of New Zealand as belonging to Australia, but in reality they are a result of the separation of an ancient landmass: millions of years ago, Gondwana, the southern half of the ancient continent of Pangaea, broke away. At that time, South America and Africa nestled together in a spooning position, with a landmass formed by modern-day India, Australia and Antarctica lying behind them. Then titanic forces inside the earth drove the crust apart: South America lost its billion-year-old contact with Africa and drifted off on a long journey westward. India broke away from the African south, leaving behind a scrap that is now called Madagascar, taking a stately route to the north in a over hundreds of thousands of years and eventually crashing into the hesitantly bobbing landmass of Asia so violently that the almost nine-kilometer high Himalayas were pushed up in the process. Meanwhile, to the south, Antarctica and Australia moved along in a tight clinch. At first they could barely keep their hands off one another, but eventually Antarctica decided on icy isolation at the South Pole and Australia took offense and sulkily headed northeast.

Antarctica was now in a hurry and rushed away, impatient for snow, ice and the evolution of the penguins – and in all its newfound haste it left its furthest, eastern tip behind. A small remnant of land on the fault line between the Australian and Antarctic plates simply refused to drown in the crackling lava of the earth's crust, bravely keeping its head above the surface of the Pacific and then striking it lucky: Aotearoa aka New Zealand is still growing.

eilig, kann Schnee, Eis und die Evolution der Pinguine kaum erwarten, schnürt mächtig davon – und lässt in all der neu gewonnenen Eile ihren äußersten, östlichen Zipfel zurück. Ein kleiner Rest Land auf der Bruchlinie zwischen australischer und antarktischer Erdplatte will und will im Lava-Knistern der Erdkruste einfach nicht untergehen, hält den Kopf zuerst tapfer über der Oberfläche des Pazifik und hat dann auch noch Glück: Aotearoa aka Neuseeland wächst immer noch.

Dass die Inseln Neuseelands ein rund 85 Millionen Jahre langes Dasein als Einsiedler hinter sich haben, weit ab von den evolutionären Entwicklungen auf anderen Kontinenten, führt zu einer bemerkenswerten Tier- und Pflanzenwelt. Neuseeland ist – ähnlich wie die Erdteile mit ähnlichem Schicksal, Australien und Madagaskar – ein evolutionäres Paralleluniversum. Hier gibt es Tiere und Pflanzen, die es anderswo nicht gibt. Und leider gilt auch die Vergangenheitsform: Es gab hier andere Pflanzen und Tiere als im Rest der Welt. Ohne echte Raubtier-Konkurrenz hatten es beispielsweise die Vögel Neuseelands nicht allzu eilig das Fliegen zu lernen, die Kakapo-Papageien, Kiwi-Sonderlinge, Takahe-Hühner und Weka-Rallen tun sich daher heute mit dem Überleben gewaltig schwer – die Moa-Laufvögel sind bereits ausgestorben. Ursache dafür war die Ankunft der Maori-Vorfahren, die den appetitlichen Großvögeln ohne jeden Fluchtinstinkt innerhalb von wenigen Jahrzehnten den Garaus machten.

Damit wären wir in der Neuzeit angekommen. Setzen einen ersten Fuß auf die Inseln Neuseelands und stellen fest: Ohne mentales Gepäck im Hinterkopf tritt man die Reise nach Aotearoa nicht an. Egal, woher man kommt, Neuseeland ist das sprichwörtliche und gefühlte Ende der Welt. Ein unwirklicher Traum, dessen pathetische Landschaften sich tief in uns verfangen haben. Dass der Filmemacher Peter Jackson seine Version des Fantasy-Epos „Herr der Ringe" auf Neuseeland inszeniert hat, kommt nicht ohne Grund. Neuseeland war und ist eben hyperreal, überlebensgroß. Seine Landschaften sind voller Magie und Eigenheit, gleichzeitig reflektieren sie beinahe archetypisch auf ganz viele andere Landschaften dieses Planeten. Die Berge Neuseelands sind bergiger als sonstwo, die Wälder dichter, die Meere tiefer und blauer, die Fjorde beängstigender, die Ebenen weiter, die Vulkane grimmiger, die Hügel sanfter und die Strände weiter. Irgendwann werden wir unseren Kindern von dieser Fahrt durch Neuseeland erzählen. Wir werden sie „40 Tage bis ans Ende der Welt" nennen. Und das ist die Wahrheit.

Neuseeland ist das sprichwörtliche und gefühlte Ende der Welt. Ein unwirklicher Traum, dessen pathetische Landschaften sich tief in uns verfangen haben. Dass der Filmemacher Peter Jackson seine Version des Fantasy-Epos „Herr der Ringe" auf Neuseeland inszeniert hat, kommt nicht ohne Grund.

New Zealand is the proverbial and perceived end of the world. An unreal dream whose awe-inspiring landscapes have become deeply ingrained in us. Filmmaker Peter Jackson had good reason to choose New Zealand to shoot.

The fact that the islands of New Zealand existed in splendid isolation for around 85 million years, far from the evolutionary developments on other continents, has produced remarkable flora and fauna. Like other landmasses with a similar history – Australia and Madagascar – New Zealand is an evolutionary parallel universe. There are animals and plants here that are not found anywhere else in the world. Unfortunately there are also downsides to this: without real competition from predators, the birds of New Zealand, for example, were in no hurry to learn to fly, so the kakapo parrot, kiwi, takahe and weka woodhen are finding it extremely difficult to survive today, while the moa is already extinct. The reason for this was the arrival of the Maori ancestors, who only took a few decades to put an end to the large, appetizing birds, which lacked any escape instinct.

This brings us to modern times. When you set foot on the islands of New Zealand for the first time, you realize that you cannot embark on the journey to Aotearoa without mental baggage on board. No matter where you come from, New Zealand is the proverbial and perceived end of the world. An unreal dream whose awe-inspiring landscapes have become deeply ingrained in us. Filmmaker Peter Jackson had good reason to choose New Zealand to shoot his version of the fantasy epic "The Lord of the Rings". New Zealand was and is hyperreal, larger than life. Its landscapes are full of magic and uniqueness, but at the same time they also echo, almost archetypically, many other landscapes on this planet. New Zealand's mountains are more mountainous than anywhere else, the forests are denser, the seas are deeper and bluer, the fjords are scarier, the plains are wider, the volcanoes are fiercer, the hills are gentler and the beaches are longer. Some day we will tell our children about this trip through New Zealand. We will call it "40 Days to the End of the World." And that will be the truth.

MOUNT COOK

MILFORD SOUND

HIGHWAY 6

HIGHWAY 60

MILFORD SOUND

MILFORD SOUND

LEWIS PASS

LINDIS PASS

MOUNT COOK

ARTHUR'S PASS

GLENORCHY

LINDIS PASS

CHRISTCHURCH
CAPE FARWELL

780 KM • 2-3 TAGE // 485 MILES • 2-3 DAYS

Türkisblau, azurblau, grasgrün. Üppige Berghänge, bewachsen mit dichten Pelzen aus fettem Gras, schieben sich unter einem endlosen Sommerhimmel zum Meer hinunter und enden in steilen Klippen über der Wasserlinie. Nach vielen tausend Kilometern ungestörten Wogens scheint der Pazifik vom plötzlichen Widerstand des Landes beinahe ein wenig überrascht.

—

Turquoise, azure, emerald. Lush mountain slopes, covered with a healthy coat of thick grass, slide casually down toward the sea under an endless summer sky, ending in sheer cliffs above the waterline. Having traveled many thousands of kilometers undisturbed, the Pacific waves almost seem a little surprised by the sudden resistance of dry land.

HIGHWAY 7

INLAND KAIKOURA ROAD

HOTEL

THE MAYFAIR
155 VICTORIA STREET
CHRISTCHURCH
WWW.MAYFAIRLUXURYHOTELS.COM

THE OBSERVATORY HOTEL
9 HEREFORD STREET
CHRISTCHURCH
WWW.OBSERVATORYHOTEL.CO.NZ

THE SALISBURY HOTEL
345 MADRAS STREET
CHRISTCHURCH
WWW.THESALISBURYHOTEL.COM

RESTAURANT

KOKOMO
20 WELLES STREET
CHRISTCHURCH
WWW.KOKOMO.NZ

CHILD SISTER
277 MANCHESTER STREET
CHRISTCHURCH

Unruhig brandet das Meer gegen diese Grenze, weiß gischtende Wellen spülen zornig über mächtige Felsbrocken. Das Wasser hinterlässt in stetig wechselndem Rhythmus Rinnsale und Bäche auf den dunkel glänzenden Steinen, strudelt aber bereits im nächsten Moment wieder darüber hinweg. Algenteppiche saugen sich voll, triefen, heben und senken sich, Luftblasen sprudeln, Muscheln öffnen und schließen vorsichtig ihre Schalen, Krebstiere staksen durch das wilde Tohuwabohu der Brandung. Der Übergang von Meer zu Land ist Konfliktzone und Paradies zugleich. Nur wenige Meter weiter oben wird alles ruhiger und klarer, Möwen surfen im Wind, Schafe sprengseln als weiße Wattebäusche die weiten Gras-Weiden der Küstenberge.

Und so beginnt unsere Reise durch Neuseeland. Mit den Bergen der Banks-Halbinsel, die sich zwischen unzähligen Buchten, klein und groß, aus dem Pazifik erheben. Aus dem All oder dem Flugzeug sieht die Banks-Halbinsel aus wie das Innere einer gigantischen Walnuss – genarbt und unruhig, aber gleichzeitig perfekt in die Hand eines Riesen passend. Man erzählt sich, der Entdecker James Cook habe die Küste für die einer echten Insel gehalten – und das war die Banks-Peninsula auch, bevor die Flüsse Waimakariri und Rakaia noch nicht das Meer in ihrem Westen zu einer riesigen Ebene aufgefüllt hatten. Mit Kies, Schotter und Geröll aus den neuseeländischen Alpen, dem von Nord nach Süd verlaufenden Hauptgebirge jener Inseln, die man Neuseeland nennt.

Wie keltische Schlangen-Ornamente oder die sich windenden Gesichts-Tattoos eines Maori ziehen die beiden Flüsse heran, flechten im Sommer schmale Rinnsale in ein breites Bett aus Geröll und werden erst am Ende des Winters für wenige Wochen zu mächtigen, grauen Strömen. Der Waimakariri fließt im Norden der Banks-Halbinsel in den Pazifik, der Rakaia in ihrem Süden. Und in ihrem Rücken, geschützt

The sea surges restlessly against the coast and white spume crashes angrily over mighty boulders. The water creates rivulets and streams on the dark, shiny stones in a constantly changing rhythm, swirling over them again and again. Dense carpets of seaweed fill with water, dripping, rising and falling. Air bubbles form, mussels open and close cautiously. Crustaceans stalk nimbly through the wild tumult of the surf. The transition from sea to land is both conflict zone and paradise at the same time. Just a few meters higher up everything becomes calmer and clearer. Seagulls surf the wind and sheep are dotted around the wide grassy pastures of the coastal mountains like tufts of white cotton wool.

This is how our journey through New Zealand begins. With the mountains of the Banks Peninsula rising from the Pacific between countless bays, large and small. In a bird's eye view, the Banks Peninsula looks like the inside of a gigantic walnut – pitted and complex, but at the same time fitting perfectly in the hand of a giant. It is said that the explorer James Cook thought that this coastline was a separate island in itself, which is exactly what the Banks Peninsula was before the Waimakariri and Rakaia rivers had turned the bay to the west into a vast plain by filling it with gravel, scree and boulders from the New Zealand Alps, the main mountain range that runs from north to south on the islands that we know as New Zealand.

Like sinuously snaking Celtic ornaments or complex Maori facial tattoos, the two rivers conjoin, weaving narrow rivulets into a wide bed of boulders in summer and only becoming mighty, gray torrents for a few weeks towards the end of winter. The Waimakariri flows into the Pacific to the north of the Banks Peninsula and the Rakaia flows to the south. Beyond, protected from the sea and nestled between the rivers, lies Christchurch. With a population of 350,000, Christchurch is the administrative capital of the Canterbury region

INLAND KAIKOURA ROAD

INLAND KAIKOURA ROAD

vor dem Meer, zwischen den Flüssen, liegt Christchurch. 350.000 Einwohner, Verwaltungssitz der Region Canterbury, das sind die technischen Daten der größten Stadt auf Neuseelands Südinsel. Christchurch hat durch die Lage auf altem Schwemmland chronisch nasse Füße, aus dem Untergrund sickern Bäche und vereinen sich nordwestlich des zentralen Hagley-Park zu einem dritten Fluss – dem Avon. Der kurvt still und dunkelgrün durchs Zentrum der Stadt, an seinen Ufern lagern sich Parkanlagen, Stege und Bootsanleger. Die Äste von Weiden tauchen ins Wasser, Kastanien und akkurat gemähte Rasenflächen säumen den Lauf des Avon, Gondeln schweben langsam unter den vielen Brücken über den Fluß dahin. Ihren Kosenamen „Garden City" trägt Christchurch also nicht umsonst, die Stadt wirkt rund um den Avon immer wieder wie aus dem Diorama einer Modelleisenbahn entstiegen – mit gemütlichen Garten-Winkeln, öffentlichen Parks und dann wieder dem typisch viktorianischen Gepräge der britischen Kolonialgeschichte. Kapitän James Cook wirft sich auf einem Denkmalsockel in die steinerne Brust und lässt den Blick über die Stadt schweifen – vermutlich gefällt ihm, was er sieht: Eine lebendige Stadt mit erkennbar traditionsreichen Wurzeln, aber ohne Scheu vor der Moderne. Immer wieder crasht moderne Architektur zwischen die traditionellen Gebäude, sorgt neuzeitlicher Pragmatismus für einen gestalterischen Tempowechsel im gemütlichen Grund-Rhythmus.

Nach Norden verebbt die Stadt ganz langsam im üblichen Stakkato von Schnellrestaurants und Autowerkstätten, dahinter schließen sich die Straßen-Quadrate von Wohnbezirken an: brusthohe Zäune in allen Schattierungen von Weiß und Braun und Grün, mit den herauslugenden Dächern niedriger Bungalows. Irgendwann ist Christchurch zu Ende, die Straße saust mehrspurig und samtglatt gestrichen voran. Vorbei an Wohngebieten, Friedhöfen, Industriegebieten, zwischen denen sich allzu nasse Wiesen oder Baumgruppen gegen das Überbautwerden wehren. Die Brücke über den Waimakariri stelzt vorsichtig über die Sandbänke und Geröllhalden dahin, zwischen denen sich der eigentliche Fluss gerade nur als harmloses Rinnsal präsentiert. Sobald die Jahreszeiten ihn wieder anschwellen lassen, wird sein Wasser aber bis zu den Deichen gehen, die den Flusslauf mit Respektabstand einhegen.

Und dann, hinter dem Fluss, sind wir wirklich unterwegs. Schnüren auf dem Highway 1 nach Norden, begleitet von Zypressen und Kiefern, von Ginster und Kuhweiden. Die Landschaft verbindet Noten von schottischen Lowlands mit einem Hauch Baskenland und einer Nase Schweden. Felder und Weiden machen sich links und rechts der Straße breit, abgeriegelt durch große Hecken. Kilometer um Kilometer geht das so, irgendwann hat das Land ein Einsehen und schiebt uns sanfte Hügel unter, die auf den nächsten Kilometern für ein wenig Unterhaltung sorgen.

and the largest city on New Zealand's South Island. The town is chronically prone to rising damp due to its location on old alluvial lands. Streams rise from the subsoil and join to form a third river – the Avon – northwest of central Hagley Park. Silent and dark, its green waters wind their way through the center of the city, with parks, footbridges and boat docks dotting its banks. The branches of willows dip into the water, sweet chestnut trees and meticulously mown lawns line the course of the Avon, gondolas cut a slow passage under the many bridges that cross the river. Christchurch's reputation as the "Garden City" is well deserved; the city on the banks of the Avon always looks like something from a model railway diorama – with secluded gardens, public parks and typical Victorian reminders of a British colonial past. Captain James Cook beats his stone breast on a monument pedestal and casts his benign gaze across the city, probably proud of the sight that meets his eyes: a lively city with clearly traditional roots, but not afraid of modernity. Contemporary architecture repeatedly elbows its way between the more traditional buildings and a modern, pragmatic approach ensures a creative variation of pace in a comfortable underlying rhythm.

To the north, the city slowly fades away into the usual scattering of fast food restaurants and car repair shops, beyond which lie the blocks of residential districts: chest-high fences in every shade of white and brown and green, with the roofs of low bungalows peeking above them. At some point Christchurch peters out entirely and the road presses ahead in multiple lanes with a velvety smooth finish. We pass residential areas, cemeteries and industrial estates, between which water-logged meadows or groups of trees defend themselves steadfastly against encroaching development. The bridge over the Waimakariri picks its way carefully over the sandbanks and scree slopes, between which the river itself only appears as a harmless trickle. As soon as the seasons swell river levels again, its water will reach the dikes that keep flooding at bay. Once beyond the river, we really start to get going, heading north on Highway 1, our progress accompanied by cypress and pine trees, gorse and grazing pastures for cattle.

The landscape combines notes of the Scottish Lowlands with a touch of the Basque Country and a hint of Sweden. Fields and pastures spread out to our left and right, enclosed by dense hedges. And so it goes on for kilometer after kilometer. At some point the country rouses from its slumber and slips a few gentle hills beneath our wheels, providing some modest entertainment over the next few kilometers. With the criss-cross pattern of meter-high pampas grass stalks on both sides, the road curves gently and winds around soft hilly slopes, then continues through the countryside. Small villages and farms line up in regimental fashion and Highway 7 over the Weka Pass entices us to venture into the hinterland for short distance. However,

INLAND KAIKOURA ROAD

FRENCH PASS

Begleitet von einem Spalier aus meterhohen Pampasgras-Wedeln wirft sich die Straße in sanfte Bögen und windet sich um weiche Hügelseiten, schnuppert dann weiter durchs Land. Kleine Dörfer und Gehöfte reihen sich hintereinander, der Highway 7 über den Weka-Pass lockt uns für einige Kilometer ins Hinterland, aber wir haben ein Ziel im Norden: Bei Goose Bay trifft der Highway 1 wieder auf den Pazifik und dahinter marschieren die Neuseeländischen Alpen bis hinunter an die Küste – das sollte spannend werden. Hinter dem breiten Schotterbett des Waiau-Uwahu-Flusses deutet das Land tatsächlich erste Geheimnisse an, ab dem Conway-Fluss geht es dann richtig los: In weiten Kehren prescht die Straße in die Berge, kurvt durch Täler und Wälder und landet dann zusammen mit dem Flusslauf des Oaro am Pazifik.

Die Küstenberge verbergen sich im sonnenglänzenden Dunst der See, das Meer schwappt mit gewaltigem Pathos an müde Kiesstrände. Wie im Traum fahren wir nun dahin, die bisherige Ruhe des Lands ist nur noch eine ferne Erinnerung. Von gemütlichem Alltag auf spektakuläre Schönheit in Sekundenbruchteilen und nun hat die Strecke den glamourösen Reiz aller Premium-Küstenstraßen der Welt: Sonne, Meer, Berge, Wind, Herrlichkeit. Aber das ist vergänglich. Nur eine Ouvertüre: An der Gooch Bay bei Kaikoura hat uns eine gemächliche Küstenebene mit dem banalen Trab von Feldern und Weiden wieder. Allerdings bäumen sich im Nordwesten nun mächtige Bergmassive mit Schneegipfeln auf, die das ganze Panorama dreidimensional und spannend machen, zu ihnen führt die Straße.

Hinter der Lagune des Lake Grassmere erreichen wir Blenheim, die erste größere Stadt seit dem mittlerweile über 300 Kilometer entfernten Christchurch. Die Stadt beginnt, wie Christchurch aufgehört hat –

our true destination lies to the north: Highway 1 rejoins the Pacific at Goose Bay, and behind it the New Zealand Alps march down to the coast – an exciting prospect. Beyond the wide gravel bed of the Waiau-Uwahu River, the country provides the first inkling of the secrets ahead, and from the Conway River onwards things really get interesting: the road rushes headlong into the mountains in wide bends, curving through valleys and forests and ending up where the Oaro River reaches the Pacific. The coastal mountains are hidden in the hazy sunshine bouncing off the sea. The waves splash moodily onto tired pebble beaches. We drive on as if in a dream, the previous peace of the countryside just a distant memory. Things switch from comfortable routine to spectacular beauty in a split second and the route takes on the glamorous appeal of all the world's premium coastal routes: sun, sea, mountains, wind, splendor. But this is a fleeting moment, just an overture: at Gooch Bay near Kaikoura we find ourselves back to a leisurely coastal plain with a banal succession of fields and pastures. However, to the northwest there are now mighty mountain massifs with snow-capped peaks that make the whole panorama seem exciting and three-dimensional. That's where we're headed.

Passing the lagoon of Lake Grassmere we reach Blenheim, the first major city since Christchurch, now over 300 kilometers behind us. The city begins just the same way that Christchurch ended – a series of low houses behind fences in all shades of a monochrome color chart. As we drift through the streets of the city center, filled with a strange nagging hunger for civilization after so many kilometers of rural conditions, we are once again overcome by the realization that we are actually on the other side of the world: Blenheim feels like a small town in Norfolk or Essex, with its single-story shops and Asian restaurants. Nail salons sit next

HOTEL

HAPUKU LODGE
STATE HIGHWAY 1
WWW.HAPUKULODGE.COM

ESCAPE TO PICTON
33 WELLINGTON STREET
PICTON
WWW.ESCAPETOPICTON.COM

FRENCH PASS

FRENCH PASS

HIGHWAY 60

HIGHWAY 60

CAPE FAREWELL

Fingernagel-Strass neben Baumarkt neben Takeaway-Fish-and-Chips – nur die opulenten Wedel von Palmen schrecken dieses Standardmotiv angelsächsischer Heimeligkeit auf. Hinter dem Wairau-Fluss im Norden von Blenheim endet die Küstenebene ein letztes Mal, hier beginnt der gebirgige Norden.

Nail salons sit next to hardware stores and fish and chip cafes – only the opulent fronds of palm trees belie this standard image of Anglo-Saxon banality. Beyond the Wairau River to the north of Blenheim, the coastal plain comes to a final end and the mountainous north begins.

mit niedrigen Häusern hinter Zäunen in allen Schattierungen eines monochromen Farbfächers. Während wir uns durch die Straßen der Innenstadt treiben lassen, nach den vielen Kilometern durchs Land mit einem kleinen, sonderbaren Hunger nach Zivilisation gefüllt, überkommt uns wieder das Gefühl, eigentlich am anderen Ende der Welt zu sein: Blenheim fühlt sich nach einer Kleinstadt in Norfolk oder Essex an, mit den einstöckigen Shops und asiatischen Restaurants. Fingernagel-Strass neben Baumarkt neben Takeaway-Fish-and-Chips – nur die opulenten Wedel von Palmen schrecken dieses Standardmotiv angelsächsischer Heimeligkeit auf. Hinter dem Wairau-Fluss im Norden von Blenheim endet die Küstenebene ein letztes Mal, hier beginnt der gebirgige Norden. Der Highway 1 schlurft noch ein paar Kilometer zwischen den Bergen dahin, landet dann in Picton am Queen Charlotte Sound – hier geht die Fähre nach Wellington auf der Nordinsel. Wir haben bereits ein paar Kilometer vorher die Reisegesellschaft gewechselt und sind nun auf dem Highway 6 unterwegs: Landen bei Havelock zum ersten Mal an den Meeresarmen der Schären- und Fjord-Küste des Nordens, schippern dann mit den Flusstälern von Te Hoiere, Rai und Ronga zielstrebig weiter.

Die heftigen Serpentinen der Ronga Road bringen uns zur Okiwi Bay und von dort schlagen wir uns an den wild bewucherten Berghängen entlang immer weiter. Kleine Straße, intime Welt, Explosion von Grün. Irgendwie kommt uns Reisenden vom anderen Ende der Welt alles altbekannt vor. In manchen Momenten könnte das hier

to hardware stores and fish and chip cafes – only the opulent fronds of palm trees belief this standard image of Anglo-Saxon banality. Beyond the Wairau River to the north of Blenheim, the coastal plain comes to a final end and the mountainous north begins. Highway 1 shuffles along between the mountains for a few more kilometers, ending up in Picton on Queen Charlotte Sound, where the ferry to Wellington on the North Island departs. We had already changed routes a few kilometers earlier and were now on Highway 6: Landing at Havelock for the first time on the archipelago and fjord-crowded inlets of the northern coast, then cruising purposefully along the river valleys of Te Hoiere, Rai and Ronga.

The sharp bends of the Ronga Road take us to Okiwi Bay. From there we continue along the wildly overgrown mountain slopes on a narrow road, our world suddenly more intimate, despite the explosion of greenery. Somehow everything seems familiar to us travelers, despite the fact that we have come from the other side of the world. Occasionally you feel like you're on a stage of the San Remo Rally, in the mountains of the Ligurian Riviera di Ponente, but then strangely unfamiliar shrubs, trees or flowers explode this Mediterranean image. The northern part of New Zealand's South Island is a world of countless inlets between islands and peninsulas. The mountain ridges with their countless small bays stretch northwards like a maze. The mainland ends at the almost

HOTEL
TE KOI
133 BRONTE ROAD EAST
BRONTE
WWW.TEKOITHELODGE.COM

RESTAURANT
ARDEN
216 HARDY STREET
NELSON
WWW.ARDEN.NZ

CAFE
JAVA HUT COFFEE
84B ARANUI ROAD
MAPUA

CAPE FAREWELL

Dass zwischen 1888 und 1912 ein Rundkopfdelfin namens Pelorus Jack Schiffe gezielt durch den French Pass gelotst haben soll, gilt als Seemannsgarn-unverdächtig – immerhin wurde „Pelorus Jack" als erster Delfin der Welt gesetzlich geschützt, ein Bronze-Denkmal in den Hängen oberhalb der strudelnden Meeresenge erinnert heute noch an diesen anrührend dienstbaren Geist des Meers.

Few people question the seafarers' yarn that a Risso's dolphin named Pelorus Jack piloted ships through the French Pass between 1888 and 1912 – after all, "Pelorus Jack" was the first dolphin in the world to be protected by law. A bronze monument in the slopes above the swirling waters Strait still reminds us today of this touchingly solicitous spirit of the sea.

eine Etappe der San-Remo-Rallye sein, in den Bergen der ligurischen Riviera di Ponente – aber dann sprengen merkwürdig unbekannte Sträucher, Bäume oder Blüten dieses mediterrane Bild. Der Norden der neuseeländischen Südinsel ist eine Welt von unzähligen Meerarmen zwischen Inseln und Halbinseln, beinahe labyrintartig ziehen sich die Bergrücken mit ihren unzähligen kleinen Buchten nach Norden. Festland-Ende liegt an der knapp 500 Meter breiten Meerenge zur Rangitoto-ki-te-Tonga-Insel, die ebenso unmöglich per Auto zu erreichen wie auszusprechen ist.

„French Pass" heißt diese Wasserstraße, der Name rührt von halsbrecherischen Querungen der Meerenge durch französische Seefahrer her. Dass sich hier die tasmanische See mit voller Gezeitenwucht in die Cook Strait presst, und bis zu zwei Meter Unterschied in Sachen Tidenhub, macht die Sache dynamisch genug. Wirklich haarsträubend wird das Ganze aber durch dicht unter der Wasseroberfläche liegende Felsen in einer kaum 100 Meter breiten Fahrrinne. Große Pötte haben hier eine nicht geringe Chance auf die eine oder andere Schramme im Rumpf – und das ist die harmlose Variante. Dass zwischen 1888 und 1912 ein Rundkopfdelfin namens Pelorus Jack Schiffe gezielt durch den French Pass gelotst haben soll, gilt als Seemannsgarn-unverdächtig – immerhin wurde „Pelorus Jack" als erster Delfin der Welt gesetzlich geschützt, ein Bronze-Denkmal in den Hängen oberhalb der strudelnden Meeresenge erinnert heute noch an diesen anrührend dienstbaren Geist des Meers.

Von diesem nördlichsten Punkt unserer Reise geht es kurvensurfend zurück zum Highway 6 und über die Whangamoa Road hinunter nach Richmond. Hier, an der Tasman Bay, haben wir noch gute 140 Kilometer bis zum Etappenende vor uns. Mit dem Highway 60 hinüber ins Takaka-Tal, vorbei an der Golden Bay und dann bis zum äußersten Zipfel der Südinsel: Cape Farewell.

500 meter wide strait to Rangitoto-ki-te-Tonga Island, which is as impossible to reach by car as it is to pronounce.

This waterway is known as "French Pass", taking its name from the crossing of the strait by foolhardy French sailors. The fact that the Tasmanian Sea pushes into the Cook Strait with full tidal force and a difference in tidal range of up to two meters makes things dynamic enough, but what makes the whole thing really hair-raising are the rocks lying just below the surface of the water in a channel that is barely 100 meters wide. Large vessels are almost guaranteed to suffer one or two scratches on the hull at the very least. Few people question the seafarers' yarn that a Risso's dolphin named Pelorus Jack piloted ships through the French Pass between 1888 and 1912 – after all, "Pelorus Jack" was the first dolphin in the world to be protected by law. A bronze monument in the slopes above the swirling waters Strait still reminds us today of this touchingly solicitous spirit of the sea.

Having reached the northernmost point of our journey we surf back to Highway 6 and down the Whangamoa Road to Richmond. Here, at Tasman Bay, we still have a good 140 kilometers to go to reach the end of the stage. We take Highway 60 over to the Takaka Valley, past Golden Bay and then to the furthest tip of the South Island: Cape Farewell.

HOTEL & RESTAURANT

DRIFT OFF GRID
1322 ABEL TASMAN DRIVE
TATA BEACH
WWW.DRIFTOFFGRID.COM

THE COURTHOUSE CAFÉ
11 ELIZABETH STREET
COLLINGWOOD

CHRISTCHURCH CAPE FARWELL

Unsere Reise über die Südinsel Neuseelands beginnt in Christchurch. Die größte Stadt des Südens liegt an der Ostküste, durch eine vorgelagerte Halbinsel gut geschützt vor dem rauen Pazifik. Die Kilometer in der flachen Küstenebene nutzen wir für ein erstes Zurechtfinden: ungewohnter Linksverkehr, der Kulturmix aus angel-sächsischen Standards und neuseeländischen Spezialitäten, die bemerkenswerte Freundlichkeit der Men-schen. Dass die ganze Zeit die Berge der neuseeländischen Alpen im Westen mit uns ziehen, erhöht unsere Vorfreude auf kommende Etappen und würzt die eher reizarme Streckenführung immer wieder. Bei Blen-heim haben wir die Berge des Nordens erreicht, hier ist der Lauf des Wairau-Flusses eine scharfe Grenze zwi-schen Schwemmebenen und bis zu 1.000 Meter hohen Bergen, die eine wild zerfaserte Küste aus Inseln, Schären und Fjorden bilden. Den Abstecher zum „French Pass" – einer gefährlichen Meerenge zwischen Fest-land und Insel – wollen wir uns nicht entgehen lassen, er sorgt zum ersten Mal andauernd und intensiv für echte CURVES-Schwingungen. Gut warmgefahren geht es dann zum Cape Farewell, einer langen Landzunge am äußersten Zipfel der Südinsel.

—

Our journey across New Zealand's South Island begins in Christchurch. The largest city in the south, it is located on the east coast, well protected from the rough Pacific by an offshore peninsula. The flat coastal plain affords us an opportunity to come to terms with our surroundings: unusual left-hand traffic, the cul-tural mix of standard Anglo-Saxon sights and New Zealand exoticism, the remarkable friendliness of the people. The fact that the mountains of the New Zealand Alps to the west follow us on our journey increases our anticipation for the coming stages and spices up what is otherwise a rather unexciting section. At Blen-heim we have reached the mountains of the north, where the course of the Wairau River forms a sharp boundary between flood plains and mountains up to 1,000 meters high in a wildly fragmented coastline of islands, skerries and fjords. We are anxious not to miss the detour to the "French Pass" – a dangerous strait between the mainland and the island - because this is the first chance to experience the continuously intense condi-tions you've come to expect from CURVES. Thoroughly warmed up, we head for Cape Farewell, a long head-land at the very tip of the South Island.

780 KM • 2-3 TAGE // 485 MILES • 2-3 DAYS

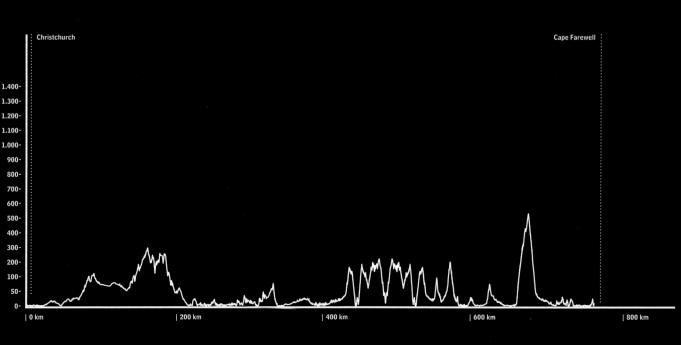

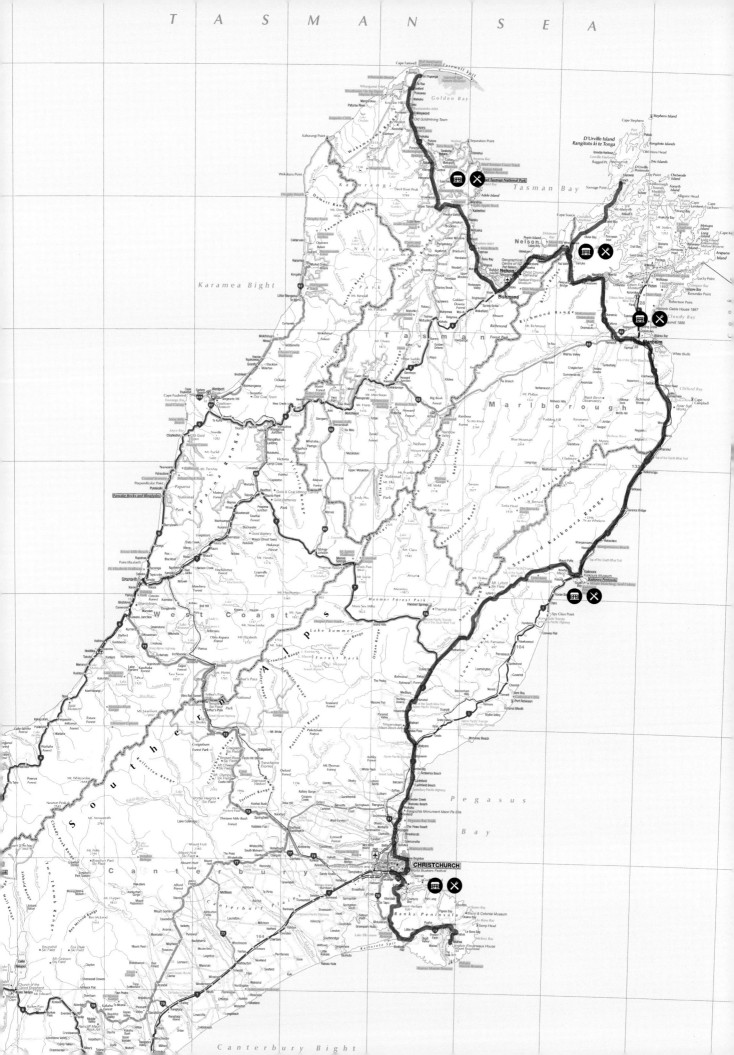

CAPE FAREWELL CHRISTCHURCH

1.150 KM • 3-4 TAGE // 715 MILES • 3-4 DAYS

Wie eine riesige Sichel liegt die Farewell-Sandbank am nördlichen Ende der Südinsel Neuseelands, so groß, dass ein Marsch zu Fuß bis an die äußerste Spitze der Dünen-Landzunge einen ganzen Tag in Anspruch nehmen würde. Das lassen wir lieber. Eine intensive Wanderung in den Klippen und Buchten am eigentlichen Cape Farewell ist eher nach unserem Geschmack.

—

The crescent-shaped Farewell sandbank lies at the northern end of New Zealand's South Island and is so large that it would take a whole day to walk to the very tip of the dune headland. That's not on our itinerary, as an intensive hike in the cliffs and bays at Cape Farewell proper is more to our liking.

Wir haben auch Glück, der Pazifik ist ruhig, die Gezeiten legen weite, vorgelagerte Sandbänke frei, in denen massige Felsriffe emporragen und sich in die vielen versteckten Einschnitte der Klippen schmiegen. Stundenlang kann man hier umherstreichen. In Spalten und Labyrinthen, Dünen und Höhlen, mit den feinen Sand-Wellenadern der letzten Flut unter den bloßen Füßen, den Nüstern voll salziger Luft und einer wirbelnden Brise in den Haaren. Die schmale Straße an der Golden Bay in Richtung Süden taumelt dann verzückt dahin, das weite Wattland der Bucht zur Linken und zur Rechten weites Grasland, in dem Scheinbuchen mit knorrigen Schirmen stehen. Warm leuchtende Sonne streift über die Horste von Tussock-Gras, macht Kiefernzweige zu Scherenschnitten. Blauer Himmel spiegelt sich in den Tümpeln aus Meerwasser im Watt, spannt sich ins Weite: Schwarze Bergketten ragen in der Ferne auf, unter Bändern von weißen Wolken.

Auf dem Highway 60 geht es dann weiter, über die Takaka-Hügel in Richtung der Tasman Bay und dann wieder zum Highway 6, zurück ins Landesinnere. Die Berge hier oben haben etwas vom herben Charme des italienischen Apennin, sind staubig und rau, lassen Lianen an moosbewachsenem Eisenholz wachsen, knirschen mit bröselnden Schieferzähnen. Silberfarnfächelndes Grün macht Nikau-Palmen Konkurrenz – die Vegetation wirkt altbekannt und gleichzeitig auf eigentümliche Weise fremdartig. Bei Westport haben wir die Westküste erreicht und

We are also lucky with our timing: the Pacific is calm, the tides reveal broad, offshore sandbanks where massive rocky reefs rise and nestle in the many hidden gashes in the cliffs. You can wander the crevices and labyrinths, dunes and caves for hours here, the fine sand from the last tide under your bare feet, your nostrils full of salt air and a buffeting breeze in your hair. The narrow road that heads along Golden Bay to the south provides a rapturously haphazard ride, with the broad mudflats of the bay to the left and wide grassland dotted with gnarled canopies of false beeches to the right. Warm sunlight illuminates the clumps of tussock grass, turning pine branches into paper cutouts. The blue sky is reflected in the pools of sea water in the mudflats, stretching into the distance: black mountain ranges rise far. The mountains here have something of the austere charm of the Italian Apennines, dusty and rough, with thick vines growing on moss-covered pōhutukawa, known as the New Zealand Christmas tree, and the familiar crunch of crumbling slate. Silvery ferns compete with palm trees for space, so that the vegetation appears familiar and strange at the same time.

We reach the west coast at Westport and there turn onto Highway 67 towards Waimangaroa. It's midday and sleek wet seals lounge on the cliffs at Cape Foulwind, plates of fish and chips are devoured by the hungry team in the city, while up at the abandoned Denniston coal mine, empty, rusting buckets swing back and forth on their cables with a barely perceptible squeal. The coast sinks into a sun-

ROAD 67

HIGHWAY 6 - FOX RIVER

65

biegen dort auf den Highway 67 in Richtung Waimangaroa ab. Es ist Mittag: Am Cape Foulwind lungern klatschnasse Seehunde auf den Klippen, in der Stadt verschwinden Fish and Chips in hungrigen Mägen und oben an der verlassenen Denniston-Kohlenmine schwingen leere, rostige Förderseilbahnen sanft quietschend hin und her. Die Küste versinkt in einem sonnendurchfluteten Traum, das weiß an lange Sandstrände gischtende Meer füttert die Luft mit glasigem Dunst. An der Mündung des Mokihinui biegt die Straße schlagartig nach Osten ins Landesinnere ab und strebt dann in die Berge hinauf. Kurvend und sich windend hechelt sie entlang üppig grüner Berghänge, vorbei am Lake Hanlon, und landet dann erneut in einem Flusstal am Meer. Moorbraun und beschaulich schlingt sich der „Little Wanganui" durch die Ebene bis zum Meer, bis zu unserem Wendepunkt am Karamea-Fluss ist es nun nicht mehr weit. „Allgäu", denken wir, „Allgäu mit Palmen und einem Küstenpanorama, das selbst Kinoleinwände zum Bersten bringen würde".

Einen gebratenen Fisch samt gegrilltem Fenchel und asiatisch eingelegtem Gemüse sowie anderthalb Stunden Fahrstrecke später sind wir zurück in Westport, zurück auf dem Highway 6. Von hier aus schlagen wir uns im Küstengebirge weiter nach Süden durch, in einem wilden Land am grau mahlenden Pazifik. Farn und holziges Gestrüpp bedeckt die felsigen Hänge, kleinwüchsige Palmenfächer und Heide gesellen sich zu diesem bunten Inferno aus Macchia durch das die Straße dahinsurft. Immer dem Rhythmus des flackernden gelben Mittelstrichs nach, unaufhörlich, Kurve um Kurve in einem hypnotischen Swing. Erst in Greymouth, an der Mündung des Grey River – oder in der Maori-Sprache Te Reo Māori auch „Māwheranui" genannt – stranden wir. Im Wortsinn. Marschieren ruhig über den weiten, grauen Felsstrand an einem tosenden, grauen Meer und können in der Ferne die weiß gekrönte Gebirgskette der Neuseeländischen Alpen ausmachen. Ein epischer Moment ist das. Die Berge so nah zu sehen. Surf and Turf. – Ausgehungert landen wir in einem Restaurant in Gehweite vom Strand und staunen nicht schlecht: Die Speisekarte ist eine Propaganda-Show für neuseeländische Küche, mit Feuerwerk, Trommelwirbel und Fanfaren. Als Goldstan-

drenched dream, the white sea spray that envelopes the long sandy beaches fills the air with glassy haze. At the mouth of the Mokihinui the road suddenly turns inland to the east and then heads up into the mountains. The curving and twisting route follows lush green mountainsides, passing Lake Hanlon, then landing again in a river valley by the sea. Brackish and calm, the "Little Wanganui" sluggishly winds its way across the plain to the sea, accompanying us almost as far as our turning point at the Karamea River. We are reminded of Germany's Allgäu region, but with palm trees and a coastal panorama that would be too much even for cinema screens.

Following a meal of fried fish with grilled fennel and Asian pickled vegetables and an hour and a half of driving, we find ourselves back in Westport and on Highway 6. From here we make our way further south, cutting a path through the coastal mountains in a wild land facing the grinding gray Pacific. Ferns and woody undergrowth cover the rocky slopes, small fan-like palms and heathers add to the colorful inferno of maquis on which the road surfs. Always following the rhythm of the flickering yellow central line, curve after curve in an incessantly, hypnotic swing. We don't stop until we reach Greymouth, at the mouth of the Gray River – or "Māwheranui" in the Maori language, Te Reo Māori. We proceed calmly across the wide gray rocky beach by a raging pearly sea, the white-tipped mountain range of the New Zealand Alps in the distance. Seeing the mountains so close is a truly epic moment: surf and turf. – Famished, we end up in a restaurant within walking distance of the beach and are amazed to find a menu like a showcase for New Zealand cuisine, with fireworks, drum rolls and fanfares. The gold standard is fluffy fish and chips casually served in a newspaper bag, smothered in an airy cloud of sophisticated mayonnaise. An Asian dream duo competes against this Anglo-Saxon classic: chicken fried in crispy tempura, smelling of sesame oil and spring onion, or grilled cauliflower with crunchy lentils. The choice is heartbreakingly difficult, so we simply choose both and, because we are already living it large, we add an incredibly fresh salmon tartare with a dollop of avocado cream. "How about a well-

HOTEL & RESTAURANT

BIRDS FERRY BOUTIQUE B&B
(GRAVEL ROAD ACESS)
163 BIRDS FERRY ROAD
WESTPORT
WWW.BIRDSFERRYLODGE.COM

VIEWS OVER TASMAN
66 HANMER TERRACE
GREYMOUTH
WWW.VIEWSOVERTASMAN.CO.NZ

BEACHVIEW MOTEL
13 MORPETH STREET
GREYMOUTH
WWW.BEACHVIEWMOTELS.CO.NZ

dard knuspern lockere Fish and Chips im lässigen Zeitungspapier-Tütchen, hoffen dabei auf ein Date mit einer luftigen Wolke aus raffinierter Mayonnaise. Gegen diesen angelsächsischen Klassiker tritt ein asiatisches Traum-Duo an: in crosser Tempura-Panade frittiertes Hühnchen, nach Sesamöl und Frühlingszwiebel duftend, oder gegrillter Blumenkohl in knackigen Linsen. Die Wahl ist herzzerreißend schwer, wir nehmen deshalb einfach beides – und weil wir schon auf großem Fuß leben, geht auch noch das unfassbar frische Lachs-Tartar unter einem Häubchen Avocado-Creme. Gut gekühlter Weißwein dazu? Ein zischend hopfiges Pale Ale?" – Das Teufelchen auf unserer rechten Schulter meint es gut mit uns. „Don't drink and drive", raunt das Engelchen auf der linken Schulter vorwurfsvoll – und es hat ja recht. Wir ordern Bergquelltafelwasser. Unter leisem Protest.

Einen kulinarischen Tagtraum später haben wir mit dieser disziplinierten Entscheidung aber unseren Frieden gemacht, denn die weitere Route fordert alle Reflexe: Am Grey River entlang geht es über den Highway 7 ins Landesinnere bis Reefton, das Land wird hügelig und wild, dann schnürt die Straße in die Täler zwischen den ersten Bergketten der neuseeländischen Alpen hinein. Speckiger, grober Asphalt zwischen dunklen Bergflanken, in deren Inneren immer noch nach Gold und Kohle gegraben wird. Hoch zum Rahu-Saddle-Pass, ein staubiger Zwischenstopp in Springs Junction, dann rüber zum Lewis-Pass. Von hier aus geht es zusammen mit Flüssen, die sich je nach Jahreszeit entscheiden, ob sie Wasser oder Geröll transportieren wollen, zum großen Lauf des Waiau Uwha. Der streift in einem weit ausladenden Bett aus Kies und Schotter bis ins Tal bei Hanmer Springs, schluckt dort den Hanmer River, presst sich dann nach einer Spontaneingebung nach Süden durch die Tekoa-Range-Bergkette und hat ab hier freie Fahrt zum Pazifik.

Dem Highway 7 ist das ab jetzt aber doch zu vorhersehbar, er bedankt sich höflich für die gemeinsame Zeit und segelt stolz in Richtung Culverden, nach Süden. Erste Zweifel an dieser Entscheidung stellen sich schnell ein, die Amuri Plains – eine hauptsächlich landwirtschaftlich genutzte Ebene zwischen dem Lauf des Waiau Uwha und

HOTELS

TOROMIRO HOTEL
52 MAIN ROAD
GOVERNORS BAY
....

RESTAURANT

SUPER
5 NORWICH QUAY
LYTTELTON
WWW.SUPER.RESTAURANT.COM
....

chilled white wine to go with it? Or maybe a zingy, hoppy pale ale?" – The little devil on our right shoulder tries to lead us into temptation. However, the little angel on our left shoulder whispers reproachfully "Don't drink and drive." Regretfully we bow to the voice of reason and order bottled mountain spring water.

One culinary daydream later, we have no regrets about this highly disciplined decision, as the rest of the route makes huge demands on all our reflexes: following the course of the Gray River we move inland on Highway 7 to Reefton. The countryside becomes hilly and wild, then the road squeezes its way into the valleys between the first mountain ranges of the New Zealand Alps. A ribbon of greasy, coarse asphalt snakes between dark mountain sides, where people are still digging for gold and coal. We climb to the Rahu Saddle Pass, a dusty stopover at Springs Junction, then cross over to Lewis Pass. From here, passing alongside rivers filled with rubble or water, depending on the season, we move on to the expansive River Waiau Uwha. It roams in a wide bed of gravel and scree down to the valley near Hanmer Springs, where it is joined by the Hanmer River. Then, in an apparent act of spontaneity, it presses south through the Tekoa Range mountain range and from here has free passage to the Pacific.

However, at this point, Highway 7 finds life too predictable, politely takes its leave and proudly sails southward towards Culverden. The first doubts about this decision quickly arise, the Amuri Plains – a mainly agricultural plain between the course of the Waiau Uwha and the Hurunui River – are rather sober. Nonetheless, after the Hurunui we can breathe a sigh of relief, because from here the journey becomes much more entertaining as we move through the low Weka Pass and beyond: gently rolling hill country spreads out in front of us, full of unassuming beauty. Shortly before Rangiora we reach the Pacific and from here the route seems familiar. Christchurch is less than 30 kilometers away and we find ourselves back where our journey began. But there is still one more thing: Christchurch is not the final destination of this stage, just a transit station. In expectant mood, we cruise further south on Highway 75, skirting the

dem Hurunui-Fluss – sind doch eher nüchtern. Hinter dem Hurunui darf aber erleichtert durchgeatmet werden, denn von hier bis weiter hinter den niedrigen Weka-Pass gestaltet sich die Reise erheblich unterhaltsamer: Ein weich schwingendes Hügelland breitet sich vor uns aus, voll sanfter Schönheit. Kurz vor Rangiora erreichen wir den Pazifik, ab hier kommt uns die Strecke bekannt vor. Christchurch liegt keine 30 Kilometer mehr entfernt, wir haben den Startpunkt unserer Reise wieder erreicht.

Einen haben wir aber noch. Christchurch ist nicht das Ziel der Etappe, sondern nur Durchgangsstation. Auf dem Highway 75 rollen wir erwartungsvoll weiter nach Süden, entlang der Küstenberge rund um die Banks-Halbinsel. Dass die weite Wasserfläche zu unserer Rechten keine ruhige Bucht des Pazifik ist, sondern ein See, merken wir erst beim Blick auf ein Schild am Straßenrand: „Lake Ellesmere" steht da, der See sei über 23 Kilometer lang und 12 Kilometer breit, mit einer mittleren Wassertiefe von knapp anderthalb Metern. Der Lake Ellesmere ist ein Produkt der Landbildung durch die geröll- und sedimenttragenden Flüsse der Gegend, gute 6.000 Jahre alt und trotz fehlender Verbindung zum nur wenige hundert Meter entfernt liegenden Meer gefüllt mit salzigem Wasser. Ruhig liegt die weite Wasserfläche da, beinahe ölig wirkt sie an manchen Stellen. Karge Grasbüschel wachsen im seichten Ufer, Insekten surren und Vogelschwärme flattern dicht über dem Wasser dahin.

Wir verabschieden uns, rollen beinahe bis zum Meer und dort haben die Küstenberge der Banks-Peninsula mit dem Lake Forsythe ein Tor gelassen, dass direkt in ihr Inneres führt. In eine kleinteilige Welt weiter Hügel, mit Hecken und Strauchreihen, mit Farmen und Weingütern – am wichtigsten aber: mit Kurven. Wir fahren ausgelassen und glücklich unter einem blauen Sommerhimmel bis zum Akaroa-Meeresarm, der dieselbe Idee hatte wie wir: vom Meer bis ins Herz der Berge gelangen. Da liegt er, der mächtige Pazifik, nach einer stürmischen Tausende-Kilometer-Reise und leckt vorsichtig und sanft an einem Kiesstrand zwischen grünen Hügeln.

Wir verabschieden uns, rollen beinahe bis zum Meer und dort haben die Küstenberge der Banks-Peninsula mit dem Lake Forsythe ein Tor gelassen, dass direkt in ihr Inneres führt. In eine kleinteilige Welt weiter Hügel, mit Hecken und Strauchreihen, mit Farmen und Weingütern – am wichtigsten aber: mit Kurven.

We say our goodbyes, moving on almost as far as the sea, where the coastal mountains of the Banks Peninsula have left a gateway in the form of Lake Forsythe, which leads directly between them. We enter a small-scale world of wide hills, with hedges and rows of bushes, with farms and wineries and – most importantly – plenty of curves.

coastal mountains around the Banks Peninsula. We only realize that the wide expanse of water to our right is a lake and not a quiet bay of the Pacific when we look at a sign on the roadside that reads "Lake Ellesmere". The lake is over 23 kilometers long and 12 kilometers wide, with an average depth of almost one and a half meters. Lake Ellesmere was formed by the area's boulder and sediment-bearing rivers, is a good 6,000 years old and, despite having no connection to the sea just a few hundred meters away, is filled with salty water. The wide expanse of water is calm, looking almost oily in some places. Sparse tufts of grass grow in the shallows, insects buzz and flocks of birds flit close to the water's surface.

We say our goodbyes, moving on almost as far as the sea, where the coastal mountains of the Banks Peninsula have left a gateway in the form of Lake Forsythe, which leads directly between them. We enter a small-scale world of wide hills, with hedges and rows of bushes, with farms and wineries and – most importantly – plenty of curves. In high spirits, we drive under a blue summer sky to Akaroa, which had the same idea as us: to get from the sea to the heart of the mountains. There it lies, the mighty Pacific, after a stormy journey of thousands of kilometers, lapping carefully and gently on a pebble beach between green hills.

RESTAURANT

5TH STREET
5 ELGIN STREET
SYDENHAM
WWW.5THSTREET.CO.NZ

TOMI JAPANESE RESTAURANT
EDGEWARE MALL
76 EDGEWARE ROAD
SAINT ALBANS
WWW.TOMI.CO.NZ

CAPE FAREWELL CHRISTCHURCH

Von ganz im Norden, bis in den westlichsten Westen, über die Berge und zurück an den Anfang: Das ist eine ganz grobe Kurzfassung der zweiten Etappe über die Südinsel Neuseelands. Wir beginnen am Cape Farewell mit seinen mächtigen Steilklippen und der sich viele Kilometer weit nach Osten krümmenden Landzunge, fahren danach in weitem Bogen rund um den Kahurangi Nationalpark und treffen am Cape Foulwind wieder auf die Westküste. Mit einem Abstecher bis Karamea entdecken wir den Norden dieser natur- und bodenschatzreichen Gegend, danach führt uns die Route hinunter nach Greymouth. Die zweite Hälfte der Etappe ist dann weniger vom Meer geprägt, sondern vom gebirgigen Landesinneren. Über das Tal des Grey River fahren wir in die Gold- und Kohlestadt Reefton, von hier aus geht es über den Rahu Saddle, Springs Junction und den Lewis Pass über den Hauptkamm der neuseeländischen Alpen. Die zeigen hier oben noch einen eher milden Charakter und ergießen viele gerölltragende Ströme nach Osten zum Pazifik. Diesen Flüssen folgen wir, drehen dann nach Süden ab und fahren zurück bis Christchurch. Das Ende der Etappe krönen wir dann mit einer Runde durch die Berge der Banks-Halbinsel, die eine Art Mini-Neuseeland an sich darstellen: Berge und Meer, Vielseitigkeit und Schönheit.

—

From the far north, to the most westerly parts, over the mountains and back to the beginning: this is a very rough summary of the second stage across the South Island of New Zealand. We start at Cape Farewell with its mighty cliffs and the headland that curves for many kilometers to the east, then drive in a wide arc around the Kahurangi National Park, meeting the west coast again at Cape Foulwind. With a detour to Karamea we discover the north of this area rich in natural and natural resources, after which the route takes us down to Greymouth. The second half of the stage is characterized less by the sea and more by the mountainous interior. We drive across the Gray River valley to the gold and coal mining town of Reefton. From here we move over the Rahu Saddle, Springs Junction and the Lewis Pass to cross the main ridge of the New Zealand Alps. Up here the mountains still seem fairly mild and benign, with many boulder-bearing streams eastwards to the Pacific. We follow these rivers, then turn south and drive back to Christchurch. We then crown the final part of the stage with a lap of the mountains of the Banks Peninsula, which are like New Zealand in miniature: mountains and sea, diversity and beauty.

1.150 KM • 3-4 TAGE // 715 MILES • 3-4 DAYS

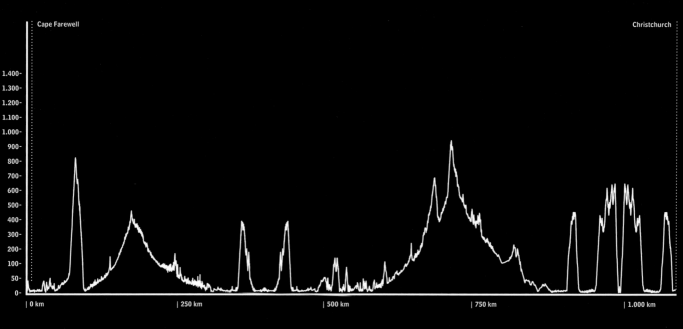

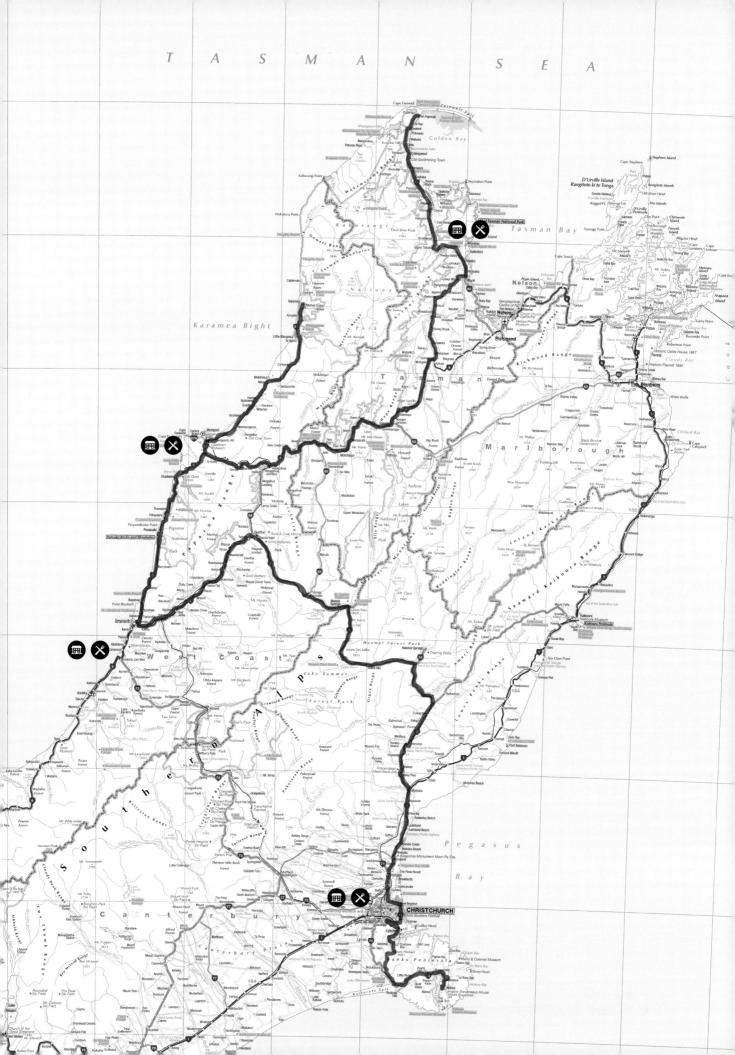

CHRISTCHURCH QUEENSTOWN

730 KM • 2-3 TAGE // 453 MILES • 2-3 DAYS

Mit dem Fahren in den Bergen ist es so eine Sache. Man beginnt im Spiel, macht dann im Flow zunehmend Ernst und hat sich zuletzt in süße Abhängigkeit gekurvt. Dass die Hügel der Banks-Halbinsel vor den Toren von Christchurch eine perfekte Einstiegsdroge sind, merken wir dementsprechend erst viel später, denn los geht es mit freudiger Leichtigkeit: Zwischen Takamatua und Akaroa schwingt die Long Bay Road spielerisch nach Osten.

—

Driving in the mountains is a very particular activity. It starts as a game, then become increasingly serious as you find yourself in the flow and finally you spiral into a delirious dependence. It takes us some time to realize that the hills of the Banks Peninsula just outside Christchurch are the perfect gateway drug, because things starts off with joyous ease: between Takamatua and Akaroa, the Long Bay Road swings playfully to the east.

ARTHUR'S PASS

ARTHUR S PASS

Wer den kleinen Abzweig vom Highway 71 in Richtung „Heritage Park" und „Eastern Bays" nimmt, hat richtig gewählt. Bereits nach wenigen hundert Meter ist die erste Anhöhe erreicht, der Blick schweift ins Weite. Ein zum Weinen schönes Landschaftsidyll breitet sich unter uns aus, mit den spiegelglänzenden Armen der Akaroa-Bay zwischen geschwungenen Hügelketten. Grüne Weiden und Berghänge sind mit gelbem Ginster und dunklen Hecken gesprenkelt, weiße Wolken fläzen an einem Himmel in unverschämt perfektem Blau. Die Straße turnt unternehmungslustig empor, wirft sich immer wieder mit frivolen Steilkurven-Andeutungen in die Kehren. Dass sich einsame Silberbuchen mit ihren strengen Baumkronen, derbe Urzeit-Farne und sogar Nikau-Palmen in das Panorama mischen, verleiht diesem Allgäu-meets-Schottland-Szenenbild einen exotischen Kick.

Nach emsiger Kletterei am höchsten Punkt angelangt, dreht die Straße bei und zieht als Summit Road nach Norden. Was eben noch bildhübsch und pittoresk war, wird jetzt magisch schön: Nadelwälder steigen in kleinen Trupps die Berghänge empor, der eben noch als vereinzelter Akzent auftretende Ginster bedeckt nun großzügig und leuchtend ganze Berghänge. Mächtige Grasbüsche neigen sich über die Straße, knorriges Buschwerk begleitet sie. Ein wucherndes Crescendo von Grün- und Brauntönen prägt diese Welt, Blätter von spitz und rasiermesserscharf bis weich und rund, derbes Geröll aus rotbraunen und schwarzen Steinen. Dazwischen tanzt ein schmales Asphaltband den Tango. Spielt den Boogie-Woogie. Swingt im Bebop. Groovt den Foxtrott. Das geht ins Blut, nicht wieder hinaus und macht Lust auf mehr.

Selbst als wir zurück am Highway 75 sind, hinter Christchurch und längst im Tal des großen Waimakariri auf träge geradeaus rollender Straße nach Nordwesten unterwegs, zuckt uns immer noch das Tanzbein. Bis Springfield müssen wir das allerdings ziemlich ruhig halten, erst ab dann ist wieder Musik drin, in dieser Fahrt. Jetzt sprintet der „Great Alpine Highway" nämlich auf steilen Rampen bergauf, schlängelt sich über den Porter's Pass bis zum Lake Lyndon. Von dort geht es über das nächste

Taking the small turnoff from Highway 71 towards "Heritage Park" and "Eastern Bays" proves to be the right choice. After just a few hundred meters we reach our first hill and the view stretches into the distance. An idyllically beautiful landscape spreads out below us, the mirror-like arms of Akaroa Bay between rolling hills. Green pastures and mountainsides are dotted with yellow gorse and dark hedges, white clouds float in a sky of outrageously perfect blue. The road rises up ambitiously, repeatedly coruscating into bends with frivolous hints of steep curves. The way that the austere treetops of lonely silver beeches rub shoulders with robust prehistoric ferns and even Nikau palms gives this Allgäu-meets-Scotland scene an exotic twist.

After a strenuous climb, we reach the highest point and the road turns around and heads north as Summit Road. What was just beautiful and picturesque now becomes quite enchanting: evergreen forests climb the mountain slopes in small groups, previously just a few isolated shrubs. The bright yellow gorse now generously covers entire mountain slopes. Mighty grasses lean over the road, interrupted by occasional gnarled bushes. This world is characterized by a rampant crescendo of green and brown tones. Leaf shapes range from pointed and razor-sharp to soft and rounded. The ground is a solid rubble made up of reddish-brown and black stones. In between, a narrow strip of asphalt dances the tango, plays boogie-woogie, swings to bebop and performs a dainty foxtrot. It insinuates itself inexorably into your blood, leaving you wanting more.

Our legs are still twitching even after we return to Highway 75 beyond Christchurch and are well into the valley of the great Waimakariri River, on a road that rolls sluggishly straight ahead to the northwest. However, we have to keep a lid on things until we reach Springfield, when the band strikes up again. At this point, the "Great Alpine Highway" sprints uphill on steep ramps, winding its way over Porter's Pass to Lake Lyndon. From there we cross to the next valley over to Arthur's Pass, then down into the valley of the Otira River. This then joins the Taramakau, another

ARTHUR'S PASS

Tal hinüber zum Arthur's Pass, dann hinunter ins Tal des Otira-Flusses. Der vertraut sich dem Taramakau an, einem weiteren dieser in breiten Geröllbetten verlaufenden Gebirgsflüssen und dessen Tal folgen wir nun für viele Kilometer weit. Immer weiter. So lange, bis wir ans nächste, große Gewässer kommen – die Pazifikküste im Westen. Rund um die Mündung des Taramakau ist nicht viel los, an der Küste versammelt sich entspannter Küsten-Lifestyle in gemächlicher Gangart: kleine Restaurants, beschauliche Siedlungen, gemütliche Lodges und Bed-and-Breakfast-Unterkünfte. An einem Kreisverkehr im Nirgendwo verabschieden wir uns vom Highway 75, er ist nach dem langen Weg über die Berge müde und übergibt seine Passagiere erleichtert dem Highway 6. Der macht es sich nun erst einmal ganz leicht, fliegt viele Kilometer weit schnurgerade am Meer entlang nach Süden. Lässt sich von der Kleinstadt Hokitika kaum ausbremsen, empfindet das Umrunden der kleinen Goldgräbersiedlung Ross vermutlich als lästige Bremsschikane für seinen Galopp am Meer entlang und muss sich dann aber zunehmend eingestehen, dass es ihm das Land inzwischen nicht mehr so leicht macht, raumgreifend voranzupreschen. Zwischen dem Lauf des Poerua und dem Lake Mapourika muss sich der Highway 6 sogar zu ein paar Serpentinen zwingen lassen – die Bergketten der neuseeländischen Alpen rücken ihm eben immer näher auf den Pelz.

Zunehmend machen sich die Berge bemerkbar, drängen auf der Bühne als eifersüchtige Hauptdarsteller nach vorn: Das breite Geröllbett des Waiho wird gespeist vom nur wenige Kilometer entfernten Franz-Josef-Gletscher. Wer die rund 10 Kilometer lange Gletscherzunge jedoch sehen möchte, muss sich hinter der Waiho-Bailey-Brücke auf einen knapp 7 Kilometer langen Fußmarsch ins Landesinnere begeben. Ebenso wie sein rund 25 Kilometer weiter südlich aus den Bergen brechender Kollege – der Fox-Gletscher – hat der Franz-Josef-Gletscher sein Eis in grauer Vorzeit direkt in den Pazifik geschoben, heute verstecken sich die zunehmend schmelzenden Eisriesen in Bergtälern. Das Land ist faszinierend: Feuchte Täler mit üppiger Vegetation sammeln sich zu Füßen des schneebedeckten Aoraki-/Mount-Cook-Massivs, mal wähnt man sich

of these mountain rivers that run in wide beds of scree, and we now follow its valley for several kilometers. We travel on and on until we come to the next large body of water – the Pacific coast in the west. There isn't much going on around the Taramakau estuary, but the coastline is host to a relaxed coastal lifestyle that follows a leisurely pace: small restaurants, tranquil settlements, cozy lodges and bed-and-breakfast businesses.

At a roundabout in the middle of nowhere we wave goodbye to Highway 75, which has grown tired after the long journey over the mountains and gratefully hands its passengers over to Highway 6. The new route takes things very easy for a while, following the sea for many kilometers, heading south. It barely breaks its stride at the small town of Hokitika, and probably finds the need to circumnavigate the small gold mining settlement of Ross to be an irritating interruption to its headlong gallop along the coast and then is increasingly forced to admit that the country no longer makes it as easy for him to rush forward in grand style. Between the course of the Poerua River and Lake Mapourika, Highway 6 is even forced to incorporate a small number of bends as the mountain ranges of the New Zealand Alps get closer and closer.

The mountains are increasingly making their presence felt, pressing forward jealously to take center stage: the wide scree bed of the Waiho is fed by the Franz Josef Glacier, just a few kilometers away. However, if you want to see the roughly 10 kilometer long glacier, you need to take a 7 kilometer hike inland beyond the Waiho-Bailey Bridge. Like its companion, the Fox Glacier, which emerges from the mountains around 25 kilometers further south, in ancient times the Franz Josef Glacier deposited its ice directly into the Pacific. These days the melting ice giants hide themselves away in mountain valleys. The countryside is quite fascinating: moist valleys filled with lush vegetation gather at the foot of the snow-covered Aoraki/Mount Cook massif. Sometimes it seems like you are on the southern side of the European Alps, while at other times towering palm trees in the undergrowth give you the feeling of being in mountain

HOTEL & RESTAURANT

TE WAONUI FOREST RETREAT
3 WALLACE STREET
STATE HIGHWAY 6
FRANZ-JOSEF-GLETSCHER
WWW.SCENICHOTELGROUP.CO.NZ

SCENIC HOTEL FRANZ JOSEF GLACIER
36 MAIN ROAD
FRANZ-JOSEF-GLETSCHER
WWW.SCENICHOTELGROUP.CO.NZ

an der Südseite der europäischen Alpen, mal sorgen im Gestrüpp aufragende Palmen für das Gefühl, in südostasiatischen Bergregionen unterwegs zu sein – wenn da nicht immer wieder die kurzen Blicke auf Gebirgsgiganten mit weiß leuchtenden Eisgipfeln wären. Und so fahren wir immer weiter, versunken in eine beinahe urzeitlich wirkende Welt mit mächtigen Silberfarnen im Urwald am Straßenrand, durch einsame Täler, in dunkelgrüne Höhen, dann wieder ans Meer hinunter. Bis zur Mündung des Haast geht das so, dann gibt der Highway 6 entnervt die Route am Ozean auf und nimmt es entschlossen mit dem Gebirge auf: Im Tal des Haast geht es flussaufwärts, und nun können wir minutiös verfolgen, wie aus dem Strom mit seinen vielen steingrauen Läufen in dem so typischen Geröllbett ein immer schmalerer, jüngerer und dynamischer Fluss wird. Als wir uns von ihm verabschieden, ist das Letzte was wir sehen, ein energisch über große Steine sprudelnder Bach aus kristallklar leuchtendem Wasser. Aus seiner Quellregion oben am Massiv des Mount Brewster hüpft aber bereits das nächste Rinnsal herab, fest entschlossen, Staub und Sand und Kies und Geröll und Felsbrocken aus den Bergen bis hinunter zum Pazifik zu befördern. Makarora heißt dieser Fluss – und er kommt nicht weit: In einem Trogtal zwischen den Bergen liegt der über 190 Quadratkilometer große Lake Wānaka, in ihm

regions of Southeast Asia – if it weren't for the constant glimpses of mountain giants with white ice peaks. And so we drive on and on, immersed in an almost primeval world of mighty silver ferns. The jungle is close enough to touch from the side of the road. We pass through lonely valleys, rising to dark green promontories, then diving back down to the sea.

And so it goes as far as the mouth of the Haast River, when Highway 6 abandons the route along the coast in exasperation and resolutely takes to the mountains: in the valley of the Haast we head upstream, allowing us follow in detail how the multitude of stone-gray rivulets in the typical scree bed become an ever narrower, younger and more dynamic river. As we turn away, the last thing we see is a stream of crystal-clear water bubbling energetically over broad stones. But the next trickle is already descending from its source up on the Mount Brewster massif, determined to move dust and sand and gravel and rubble and boulders from the mountains down to the Pacific. This river is called Makarora – and is relatively short, disappearing into Lake Wānaka, which measures over 190 square kilometers in size and lies in a trough between the mountains. Somehow the river made it down to the sea, despite the fact that the deepest part of the lake

CARDRONA VALLEY ROAD

verschwindet der Makarora. Und irgendwie hat es der Fluss damit doch bis zum Meer hinunter geschafft, denn die tiefste Stelle des Sees liegt rund 20 Meter unter dem Meeresspiegel des Pazifik. In direkter Nachbarschaft des Lake Wānaka, nur ein Tal weiter und nach wenigen Kilometern Fahrt über den Bergsattel „The Neck" zu erreichen, liegt der Lake Hawea. Ein majestätisches Juwel aus blau leuchtendem Wasser zwischen dunklen Bergketten, dessen Ränder ein Saum aus saftigen, grünen Grasmatten umgibt. Am südlichen Ufer des Sees rollen wir in Hawea aus – nach so vielen Kilometern Fahrt durch einsames Land fühlt sich das kaum 2.000 Einwohner fassende Dorf an wie eine Stadt. Auftanken, durchatmen, Puls runterregeln. Noch etwas über 80 Kilometer bis zum Ende der Etappe, die wir auf leichtem Fuß angehen. Mit gelassenem Ruhepuls durch ein vielseitiges und buntes Land, hinunter nach Albert Town und Wānaka am Südufer des Lake Wānaka, dann zu Füßen des Mount Cardrona immer weiter durchs Cardrona Valley nach Süden.

Am Mount Rock Peak klettert die Straße in einem engen Tal steil hinauf, gräbt sich energisch in die Bergflanken, landet am Ende auf dem Crown Range Summit – und spätestens jetzt hat der „Herr der Ringe"-Fan in uns endgültig Schnappatmung: Für die Drehorte im Norden der Südinsel hätte man oben am Takaka Hill, am Mount Olympus oder Mount Owen noch mehrstündige Bergwanderungen hinlegen müssen, hier unten an der Crown Range ist ein Gänsehaut-Blick hinein in die Cinemascope-Landschaften der Fantasy-Filme problemlos direkt neben der Straße möglich.

Nach einer Schussfahrt auf langen Pass-Rampen und schließlich energischen Serpentinen mit Ausblick in die vor uns liegende Ebene des Lake Hayes haben wir den Karawau-Fluss erreicht – „Herr der Ringe"-Nerds kennen die Gegend rund um das Chard-Farm-Weingut als die „Säulen der Könige" am „Anduin". Über Wilcox Green und Arrowtown machen wir die Reise nach Mittelerde komplett und landen am Ende der Etappe in Queenstown. Aber die Stadt wird uns nicht lange halten, wir sind Gefährten, stehen ganz im Bann des einen Rings: Soulful Driving.

is around 20 meters below Pacific sea level. Lake Hawea is located right next to Lake Wānaka, just one valley over and after a few kilometers drive over the mountain saddle known as "The Neck". This is a majestic jewel of lustrous blue water, glowing between dark mountain ranges, its edges fringed by mats of lush green grass. On the southern bank of the lake we roll into the settlement of Hawea.

After so many kilometers of driving through lonely countryside, the village of barely 2,000 inhabitants feels like a city. Time to recharge our batteries, inhale deeply and regulate our heart rate. We still have a little over 80 kilometers to go until the end of the stage. We're planning to take this section gently, with a relaxed, resting pulse as we glide through varied and colorful countryside, down to Albert Town and Wānaka on the southern shore of Lake Wānaka, then further south through the Cardrona Valley at the foot of Mount Cardrona.

The road climbs steeply up a narrow valley at Mount Rock Peak, digging energetically into the mountain sides and ending up on the summit of the Crown Range. Finally, the "Lord of the Rings" fan in us is left gasping for air: it took several hours for the film crew to hike to locations on Takaka Hill, Mount Olympus or Mount Owen in the north of the South Island, but down here on the Crown Range you can easily get a jaw-dropping view of the Cinemascope landscapes of the fantasy film series right next to the road.

After negotiating long mountain pass climbs and energetic switchbacks with a view of the plain of Lake Hayes ahead of us, we reached the Karawau River.

"Lord of the Rings" nerds know the area around the Chard Farm winery as the "Pillars of Kings" on the fictional River Anduin. We complete the journey to Middle-Earth via Wilcox Green and Arrowtown and end up in Queenstown at the end of the stage. However, the city won't detain us for long, we are a fellowship, completely under the spell of the one ring: Soulful Driving.

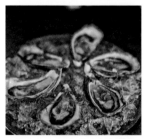

HOTEL & RESTAURANT

SHERWOOD
554 FRANKTON ROAD
QUEENSTOW
WWW.SHERWOODQUEENSTOWN.NZ

MUTTONBIRD
33 ARDMORE STREET
WANAKA
WWW.MUTTONBIRD.CO.NZ

KIKA
2 DUNMORE STREET
WANAKA
WWW.KIKA.NZ

CHRISTCHURCH QUEENSTOWN

Auch auf der dritten Etappe überqueren wir die Südinsel Neuseelands und die Bergkette der neuseeländischen Alpen einmal komplett, von Ost nach West. Mit einer Fahrt über die bildschöne Banks-Halbinsel fahren wir uns zuerst warm und machen uns dann auf den langen Weg durch die Ebene des Waimakariri-Flusses nach Westen. Über den Porters Pass und Castle Hill dringen wir ins Innere des Gebirges vor, treffen am Arthurs Pass erneut auf den Waimakariri und fahren dann am Fuß des Mount Temple zur Westseite der Alpen. Mit dem Flusstal des Taramakau gelangen wir zum Pazifik und haben nun viele Kilometer am Meer vor uns. Ausgebremst wird die Route an der Küste entlang immer wieder durch große Flüsse, die in ausladenden Betten große Mengen Geröll aus den Bergen heruntertragen: Der Mikonui, der Waitaha, der Wanganui, der Poerua und schließlich der Whataroa. Es folgen die Schmelzwasserabflüsse des Franz-Josef-Gletschers und des Fox-Gletschers – bei Haast verlassen wir diese wilde Küste endgültig. Über den River Haast geht es nun in die Berge hinein, bis zu den Trogtälern des Lake Wānaka, und Lake Hawea. Und hier haben wir nun das im Süden anschließende Cardrona Valley sowie die Crown Range am Übergang in Richtung Queenstown erreicht.

—

On the third stage we once again cross the South Island of New Zealand and the mountain range of the New Zealand Alps completely, moving from east to west. We first warm up with a drive across the beautiful Banks Peninsula and then set off on the long journey west through the plain of the Waimakariri River. We advance into the interior of the mountains via Porters Pass and Castle Hill, encountering the Waimakariri again at Arthurs Pass and then driving to the western side of the Alps in the shadow of Mount Temple. The Taramakau river valley ushers us to the Pacific and we now have many kilometers of coastline ahead of us. The route along the coast is repeatedly interrupted by major rivers that carry large amounts of rubble down from the mountains in broad beds: the Mikonui, the Waitaha, the Wanganui, the Poerua and finally the Whataroa. We then come upon the meltwater outflows of the Franz Josef Glacier and the Fox Glacier. We finally leave this wild coast at Haast. Crossing the River Haast, we now enter the mountains, driving as far as the trough-like valleys of Lake Wānaka and Lake Hawea. We have now reached the Cardrona Valley in the south and the Crown Range as we swing towards Queenstown – from here, "Lord of the Rings" fans will be in seventh heaven thanks to the many locations used in the filming of the fantasy saga down here.

730 KM • 2-3 TAGE // 453 MILES • 2-3 DAYS

GLENORCHY

QUEENSTOWN INVERCARGILL

700 KM • 2-3 TAGE // 434 MILES • 2-3 DAYS

„O Lórien, klar ist das Wasser in deinem Quell, weiß der Strom in weißer Hand, schöner noch sind Laub und Land in Lórien als die Gedanken der Sterblichen." – Diese Liebeserklärung an eine imaginäre Landschaft legt „Herr der Ringe"-Autor J.R.R. Tolkien seinem Zauberer Gandalf über das Elbenland Lothlórien in den Mund – und wer am Ufer des Lake Wakatipu von Queenstown bis nach Glenorchy an der Mündung des Dart River fährt, ahnt schnell, weshalb Kult-Regisseur Peter Jackson seine „Herr der Ringe"-Verfilmung auf Neuseeland durchziehen musste.

—

"O Lórien! Clear is the water of your well; white is the star in your white hand; unmarred, unstained is leaf and land in Dwimordene, in Lórien, more fair than thoughts of Mortal Men." – "Lord of the Rings" author J.R.R. Tolkien places this declaration of love to an imaginary landscape in the mouth of the wizard Gandalf, speaking about the Elven land of Lothlórien. Anyone who drives along the shores of Lake Wakatipu from Queenstown to Glenorchy at the mouth of the Dart River will soon understand why cult filmmaker Peter Jackson couldn't help but choose to shoot his "Lord of the Rings" fantasy film series in New Zealand.

GLENORCHY

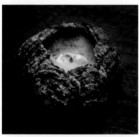

HOTEL & RESTAURANT

ROSEWOOD MATAKAURI'S
FARRYCROFT ROW
569 GLENORCHY ROAD
QUEENSTOWN
WWW.ROSEWOODHOTELS.COM

AMISFIELD
10 LAKE HAYES ROAD, RD 1
QUEENSTOWN 9371
ARROWTOWN 9351
WWW.AMISFIELD.CO.NZ

Die idyllische Heimat der „Hobbits" auf der Nordinsel und die epischen Landschaften der Wanderungen, Schlachten und mystischen Elbenreiche hier unten auf der Südinsel: Mächtige Bergrücken drängen aus der Erdkruste, ragen in einen gläsernen Himmel in Weiß und Blau hinauf. Krause Felder aus dichtem, grünem Buschwerk bedecken die Sockel, braun leuchtende Farn- und Gras-Matten die Hänge, kahle und beinahe schwarze Felskuppen machen die Schöpfe aus. Dahinter stehen mächtige Felsriesen Spalier: Berg-Titanen mit beinahe überirdisch gleißenden Gipfeln aus Eis und Schnee. Graugrüne Flüsse wogen aus den Bergen herunter, schlängeln sich zwischen Geröll und Sandbänken dahin, die sie in jahrzehntelanger Arbeit aufgeschichtet haben.

Das kleine Glenorchy duckt sich beinahe schüchtern in diese Szenerie am nördlichen Ende des Lake Wakatipu, legt sein in Quadraten angelegtes Straßennetz friedlich in die Auen am Talboden: kleine Holzhäuser umgeben von sauber gemähtem Rasen, auf dem fremd wirkende Palmen eine perfekte Schottland-Illusion crashen, die dem Städtchen vermutlich seinen Namen eingetragen hat. Die Freundlichkeit der Menschen ist umwerfend, wie beinahe überall auf Neuseeland werden Reisende interessiert nach dem Woher-und-Wohin gefragt, beim Vorbeifahren winkt und grüßt es von den Gehwegen. Einfach so. In den gemütlichen Pubs warten Tresen mit mächtigen Zapfhähnen auf Durstige, charmante Lädchen laden zum Stöbern ein: Seife aus Schafsmilch, riesige Gläser mit bunten Bonbons auf der Kassentheke, ein Arrangement aus derben Lederhüten gegen die Sonne. Regionale Käsesorten in summenden Kühlregalen, daneben eine Sammlung sichtlich handgenähter Plaids sowie ganz und gar nicht handgemachter chinesischer Plastik-Spielwaren. Honig und Bienenwachskerzen, selbstgemachte Limonade und Mini-Duftkissen für den Kleiderschrank, knorrige Maori-Schnitzereien und sauber gestapelte T-Shirts mit Erinnerungsaufdruck für Touristen. I love Glenorchy/Otago. Wir auch.

Mit wässrigem Mund stehen wir vor Glasvitrinen in denen Brocken von Salz-Karamell

The North Island provided an idyllic home for the hobbits, while the South Island supplied epic backdrops for treks, battles and mystical elven kingdoms: mighty mountain ridges push up from the earth's crust, rising into a glassy sky in white and blue. Curling fields of dense, green brush cover the lower reaches, while glowing mats of brown ferns and grass cling to the upper slopes and bare, almost black rocky outcrops top the hills. Beyond them stand mighty rock giants: mountainous titans with almost unearthly glistening peaks of ice and snow. Grey-green rivers surge down from the mountains, meandering between boulders and sandbanks that have built up over decades.

The small town of Glenorchy slips almost shyly into this scene at the northern end of Lake Wakatipu, peacefully spreading its grid of streets on the meadows of the valley floor: small timber houses surrounded by neatly mown lawns where foreign-looking palm trees subvert the otherwise perfect illusion of Scotland, which probably gave the town its name. Like almost everywhere in New Zealand, the people are amazingly friendly: travelers are asked with interest where they have come from and where they are going, and people wave and say hello from the sidewalks as they drive past. That's just how life is here. Bar counters with powerful taps await the thirsty in the cozy pubs. Charming little shops invite you to browse: soap made from sheep's milk, huge jars of colorful candies at the checkout, an arrangement of sturdy leather hats to protect against the sun. Regional cheeses sit on humming refrigerator shelves. A collection of clearly handmade plaids rub shoulders with definitely not handmade plastic toys from China. You'll find honey and beeswax candles, homemade lemonade and mini scented sachets for the wardrobe, as well as gnarled Maori carvings and neatly stacked commemorative tourist T-shirts. I love Glenorchy/Otago. Us too.

We stand in front of glass display cabinets with our mouths watering, staring at chunks of salted caramel and ranks of blueberry muffins, while chicken kimchi wraps provide an exotic touch. Finally, we end up with a large cup of latte into which we dip raisin rolls. We sit, people watch, listen to the chatter of visitors streaming in and out, letting

neben Blaubeer-Muffins warten sowie Hühn-chen-Kimchi-Wraps für eine exotische Note sorgen – und landen am Ende dann doch bei einer großen Tasse Milchkaffee, in die wir Rosinenschnecken tunken. Sitzen, Leute beobachten, dem Geplapper der herein- und hinaus-strömenden Besucher lauschen, die Zeit verstreichen lassen. Besser geht's nicht. Außer: weiterfahren. Die Straße am Seeufer zurück nach Queenstown hinunter, gute 50 Kilometer weit, während sich dunkle Wolken über den Bergen orange vom Sonnenlicht färben und das Wasser des Lake Wakatipu geheimnisvoll türkisgrün leuchtet.

Bei Queenstown formt der See ein Knie nach Osten, zieht dann aber wieder mit strengem Südkurs weiter, die Straße schneidet hier eine Trasse ins steil zum Wasser abfallende Seeufer. Erst hinter dem Aussichtspunkt zum Devils Staircase öffnet sich das Tal und die Ufer rücken etwas weiter ab. Bei Kingston läuft der riesige See an seinem südlichsten Punkt aus, beinahe 100 Kilometer weit hatten wir ihn wie einen Fjord an unserer Seite. Plötzlich ohne die enorme Wasserfläche zur Rechten zu sein, fühlt sich sonderbar an, die Bergketten links und rechts des Tals, in dem wir unsere Fahrt weiter fortsetzen, wirken ohne den See regelrecht verloren. Als fehle ein entscheidendes Element. Und an der kleinen Kreuzung der Highways 6 und 97 lassen uns auch die Berge im Stich: Am Five Rivers Cafe geht es nach Westen, in die weite Ebene hinein, die sich von hier bis hinunter nach Invercargill zieht.

Unser Plan ist klar: rüber zum Highway 94 fahren und dem dann bis zum Fuß der Berge im Westen folgen. Also den Tempomat einlegen, das Radio aufdrehen und bei gelassen groovendem Reisetempo ins Meilenfresser-Paralleluniversum einklinken. Zum Oreti-River, dann durch die Hügel der Red Tussock Conservation ins Tal des Mararoa rollen. Durch weites Land, in dem uns trotz der ständigen Begleitung durch Felder und Weiden kaum eine Menschenseele begegnet. Die eigentlichen Bewohner des Landes bleiben lange unter dem Radar unserer Wahrnehmung, obwohl sie sich alle Mühe geben, diesen blinden Fleck zu ver-

the time pass. Things don't get any better. However, we need to keep driving. We beetle down the lakeside road back to Queenstown, a good 50 kilometers away, while dark clouds over the mountains turn orange in the sunlight and the water of Lake Wakatipu glows a mysterious turquoise green.

At Queenstown, the lake bends to the east, but then continues again on a strictly southerly course; the road here cuts a route into the lake shore, which slopes steeply down to the water. It is only after we pass the Devil's Staircase lookout point that the valley opens up and the banks move back a little further. The huge lake ends at its southernmost point near Kingston. By this time we have traveled almost 100 kilometers along its fjord-like edges. It suddenly feels strange not having the enormous body of water on the right; the mountain ranges to the left and right of the valley through which we continue our journey seem quite lost without the lake, as if a crucial element was missing. Even the mountains abandon us at the small intersection of Highways 6 and 97: at the Five Rivers Cafe we head west into the wide plain that stretches from here all the way down to Invercargill.

We have a clear plan: we're going to drive over to Highway 94 and then follow it to the foot of the mountains to the west. So, we engage cruise control, turn up the radio and join the mile-munching parallel universe at a relaxed, grooving cruising speed. We reach the Oreti River, then roll through the hills of the Red Tussock conservation area into the Mararoa Valley. We pass through this vast countryside meeting hardly a soul, despite the signs of human intervention in fields and pastures. The actual inhabitants of the country remain under our radar for a long time, although they make every effort to leave their mark: things start with occasional small bites then progress to the irritated waving of hands – and at some point the first black fly gets stuck in your teeth. By now the little tormentors are everywhere. Again and again they lure us out of our reserve with short, painful test bites until we simply refuse to leave the car anymore. Little buggers, we think, rolling up the

SCENIC FLIGHTS

TRUE SOUTH FLIGHTS LTD
1B/8 12 HAWTHORNE DR,
FRANKTON, QUEENSTOWN
WWW.TRUESOUTHFLIGHTS.CO.NZ

HOTEL & RESTAURANT

MILFORD SOUND LODGE
STATE HIGHWAY 94
MILFORD SOUND
WWW.MILFORDLODGE.COM

lassen: Es beginnt mit kleinen Stichen bei kurzen Pausen, geht mit genervtem Händewedeln weiter – und irgendwann gerät uns die erste Kriebelmücke sogar zwischen die Zähne. Spätestens jetzt sind die kleinen Quälgeister omnipräsent. Immer wieder locken sie uns mit kurzen, schmerzhaften Probebissen aus der Reserve, bis wir das Auto einfach nicht mehr verlassen. Mistviecher, denken wir, fahren die Scheiben hoch und machen entschlossen Kilometer, um das Mücken-Territorium schnellstmöglich hinter uns zu lassen. Am Lake Te Anau angekommen, haben wir die Attacken dieser ungewohnt unfreundlichen Locals beinahe vergessen. Jetzt beginnen die Berge des Fjordland National Park, der seinen Namen nicht umsonst trägt: Die Seitenarme des Te-Anau-Sees oder Manapouri-See reichen wie Fjorde weit verästelt in die Bergtäler hinein, schneebedeckte Gipfel ragen über schwarzem Wasser auf. Nur die sternförmigen Büschelkronen von Cabbage-Tree-Palmen erinnern uns daran, dass wir nicht in Skandinavien gelandet sind, sondern am ganz anderen Ende der Welt.

Übrigens – „Palme" stimmt nicht wirklich. Die nur in Neuseeland beheimateten Bäume mögen zwar aussehen wie Yucca-Palmen auf Stelzen, haben aber rein evolutionär betrachtet eine andere Entwicklung hinter sich. Wer es ganz genau wissen will, sollte sich vor dem Studium des Natur-Lexikons übrigens eine Flasche guten neuseeländischen Weins aufmachen und etwas Zeit mitbringen, die Sache ist nicht ganz unkompliziert: Yucca und Cabbage Tree gehören – Überraschung – zu den Spargelgewächsen. Während die Yucca-Palme (die keine Palme ist ...) hier aber die Ordnungs-Abzweigung zu den Agaven nimmt, hat es den Cabbage Tree (oder auf Maori: Tī Kōuka) zu den „Keulenlilien" verschlagen. Nie gehört? – Das ist in Neuseeland nicht so unüblich, ein paar Hunderttausend Jahre Trennung vom Rest der Welt lösen evolutionär betrachtet einiges an Sonderwegen aus.

windows and determinedly driving many kilometers in an effort to leave mosquito territory behind as quickly as possible. By the time we arrive at Lake Te Anau, we have almost forgotten the attacks from these unusually unfriendly locals. Now the mountains of the Fiordland National Park begin. The park truly deserves its name: the branches of Lake Te Anau or Lake Manapouri extend like fjords far into the mountain valleys, snow-covered peaks rise above black water. Only the star-shaped tufted crowns of cabbage tree palms remind us that we are not in Scandinavia, but at the very other end of the world. By the way – "palm tree" isn't really correct. The trees, which are only native to New Zealand, may look like yucca palms on stilts, but from a purely evolutionary perspective they have had a different development. If you want to know exactly, you should open a bottle of good New Zealand wine and take some time to study the lexicon of local flora. This is by no means a simple issue: surprisingly, the yucca and cabbage tree are members of the asparagus family. While the yucca palm (which is not a palm tree at all...) is a type of agave, the cabbage tree (or in Maori: Tī Kōuka) is related to "club lilies". Never heard of them? – That's nothing unusual in New Zealand, as a few hundred thousand years of separation from the rest of the world has resulted in a number of special paths from an evolutionary perspective.

The long road north, to Milford Sound, feels almost the same: we find ourselves driving into a landscape divorced from the rest of the world in a kind of dream-state. Bold mountains, dark fjords, breathtaking panoramas. When you're inland it's hard to believe that the almost 16 kilometer long Milford Sound is an arm of the Pacific. But the "Scandinavian feel" of Lake Te Anau is now gone: there are no mountain cones, rocky ridges and ice giants to the north; instead, you get the feeling of being on a completely different planet. The landscape features special effects that you wouldn't dare

Der lange Weg nach Norden, zum Milford Sound, fühlt sich beinahe genauso an: Wir fahren in eine von der Welt abgetrennte Landschaft hinein, die dort oben vor sich hinträumt. Kühne Berge, dunkle Fjorde, atemberaubende Panoramen. Dass der beinahe 16 Kilometer lange Milford Sound ein Meeresarm des Pazifik ist, kann man im Landesinneren kaum glauben. Die „Skandinavien"-Assoziation des Lake Te Anau ist aber dahin: Solche Bergkegel, Felsgrate und Eisriesen gibt es im Norden eher nicht, stattdessen beschleicht einen immer wieder das Gefühl auf einem ganz anderen Planeten unterwegs zu sein. Die Landschaft ergeht sich in Special Effects, die man sich in einem Film kaum trauen würde, um nicht unglaubwürdig zu wirken. Gischtende Wasserfälle tauchen aus unfassbaren Höhen auf und treffen beinahe nur noch als Sprühnebel die Oberfläche des Wassers. Mächtige Felsformationen lagern sich vor jähen Felsabstürzen – daneben fällt glasklares Wasser weiter in dunkelgrüne Finsternis. Mit grünem Pelz bedeckte Berge legen sich Kragen aus Wolkenringen um. – Wir staunen. Und staunen.

Den Rückweg hinunter nach Te Anau und weiter bis zum Mararoa-Fluss fahren wir in andächtigem Schweigen, zum Abschied haut die Natur noch einmal kräftig auf die Pauke: Eine mächtige Wolkendecke hat sich über das Land gelegt, feine Lücken lassen Sonnenstrahlen hindurchdringen, die wie Suchscheinwerfer über die Ebene rasen. Dramatisch.

Zusammen mit dem Waiau zielen wir schnurgerade nach Süden, wir sind beinahe froh, dass uns die Landschaft nun eine emotionale Pause gönnt: Aus dem Schönheits-Crescendo der Berge ist der bodenständige Trab einer Straße zwischen Feldern geworden, der Telefon- und Stromleitungen in stetigem Auf-und-Ab folgen. Auf und ab. Wie die Wellen unten an der Südküste auf dem Weg nach Invercargill.

Die Landschaft ergeht sich in Special Effects, die man sich in einem Film kaum trauen würde, um nicht unglaubwürdig zu wirken. Gischtende Wasserfälle tauchen aus unfassbaren Höhen auf und treffen beinahe nur noch als Sprühnebel die Oberfläche des Wassers. Mächtige Felsformationen lagern sich vor jähen Felsabstürzen – daneben fällt glasklares Wasser weiter in dunkelgrüne Finsternis.

The landscape features special effects that you wouldn't dare to use in a movie because they seem so unbelievable. Misty waterfalls appear from incredible heights and almost only hit the surface of the water as spray. Mighty rock formations stretch before sudden rock falls – next to them, crystal-clear water tumbles onward into fathomless green darkness.

to use in a movie because they seem so unbelievable. Misty waterfalls appear from incredible heights and almost only hit the surface of the water as spray. Mighty rock formations stretch before sudden rock falls – next to them, crystal-clear water tumbles onward into fathomless green darkness. Green-clad mountains are wrapped with collars of cloud. We are amazed. Over and over again.

We complete the return journey to Te Anau and onward to the Mararoa River in reverent silence, as we say goodbye, nature strikes up the drum once again: a mighty blanket of clouds has settled over the land with narrow gaps allowing the sun's rays to penetrate like searchlights racing across the plain. So dramatic. Following the Waiau we head straight south, almost glad that the landscape is giving us an emotional break: the crescendo of the mountains' beauty has reduced to a down-to-earth trot between fields, with telephone and power lines as constant companions. Up and down we go, like the waves down on the south coast on the way to Invercargill.

QUEENSTOWN INVERCARGILL

Die Fjord-artigen Seen Wakatipu und Te Anau prägen die erste Hälfte dieser Etappe. Im Norden des Lake Wakatipu kommen Fans der „Herr der Ringe"-Verfilmung auf ihre Kosten: Der von Glenorchy aus zu sehende Mount Earnslaw eröffnet „Die zwei Türme", das reale Landschaftsdouble des Film-Elbenreichs Lothlórien findet sich ebenfalls hier oben. Weitere Drehorte liegen rund um Queeenstown: Wilcox Green und Arrowtown. Aber auch im Süden geht das Fest für Film-Fans weiter, der Waiau River zwischen Te Anau und Manapouri wurde von Regisseur Peter Jackson zum Film „Anduin" erklärt, die Wälder an der Takaro Road hinter Te Anau zum „Fangorn"-Wald aus dem Fantasy-Epos. Natürlich müssen aber auch Reisende, die keine Fan-Beziehung zu Buch oder Film aufgebaut haben, nicht auf cineastische Momente verzichten. Die vielseitigen Landschaften der neuseeländischen Südinsel sind so spektakulär, dass man sich keine Hobbits, Orks und Elben in sie hinein vorzustellen braucht, um immer wieder von ihrer Schönheit berührt zu werden. Ein erster Höhepunkt ist der Besuch des Milford Sound – einem vom Pazifik über 15 Kilometer ins Landesinnere hineinragenden Fjord. In seinen Gewässern leben Delfine, Seehunde und Zwergpinguine, unter den Berg-Charakterdarstellern an seinen Ufern ist besonders der steil aufragende Mitre Peak zu nennen. Eine ähnlich Fjord-artige Landschaft macht die Umgebung des Lake Te Anau aus, der allerdings keine Verbindung zum Pazifik besitzt und lediglich durch die vielen Seitenarmen in das Gebirge seinen Fjord-Charakter bekommt. Von hier aus führt die Route dann hinunter an die südlichste Küste Neuseelands, bei Invercargill.

The fjord-like lakes Wakatipu and Te Anau dominate the first half of this stage. In the north of Lake Wakatipu, fans of the "Lord of the Rings" film series will be in seventh heaven: Mount Earnslaw, which can be seen from Glenorchy, provides the opening shots for "The Two Towers", and the real landscape double of the elven kingdom of Lothlórien can also be found up here. Other filming locations can be found around Queenstown: Wilcox Green and Arrowtown. However the treat for film fans also continues in the south, the Waiau River between Te Anau and Manapouri was used as the "Anduin" by director Peter Jackson, while the forests on Takaro Road behind Te Anau served as the "Fangorn" forest from the fantasy epic. Of course, even travelers who are not (yet) fans of the books or movies can still enjoy the cinematic moments. The diverse landscapes of New Zealand's South Island are so spectacular that you don't need to imagine hobbits, orcs and elves in them to be constantly touched by their beauty. A first highlight is a visit to Milford Sound – a fjord that extends over 15 kilometers inland from the Pacific. Dolphins, seals and dwarf penguins live in its waters, and the steep Miter Peak is particularly notable among the mountains on its banks. A similar fjord-like landscape is found in the surroundings of Lake Te Anau, which, however, is not connected to the Pacific and only looks like a fjord because of the many branching arms in the mountains. From here the route leads down to the southernmost coast of New Zealand, near Invercargill.

700 KM • 2-3 TAGE // 434 MILES • 2-3 DAYS

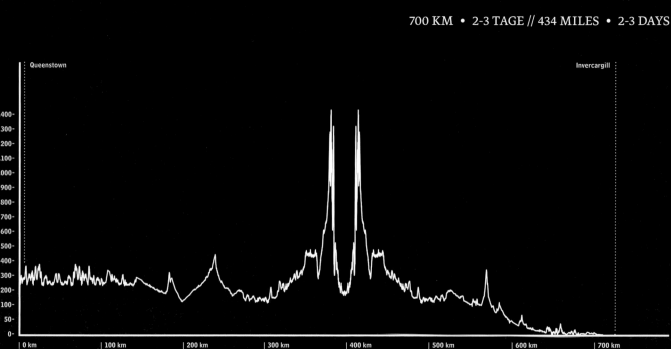

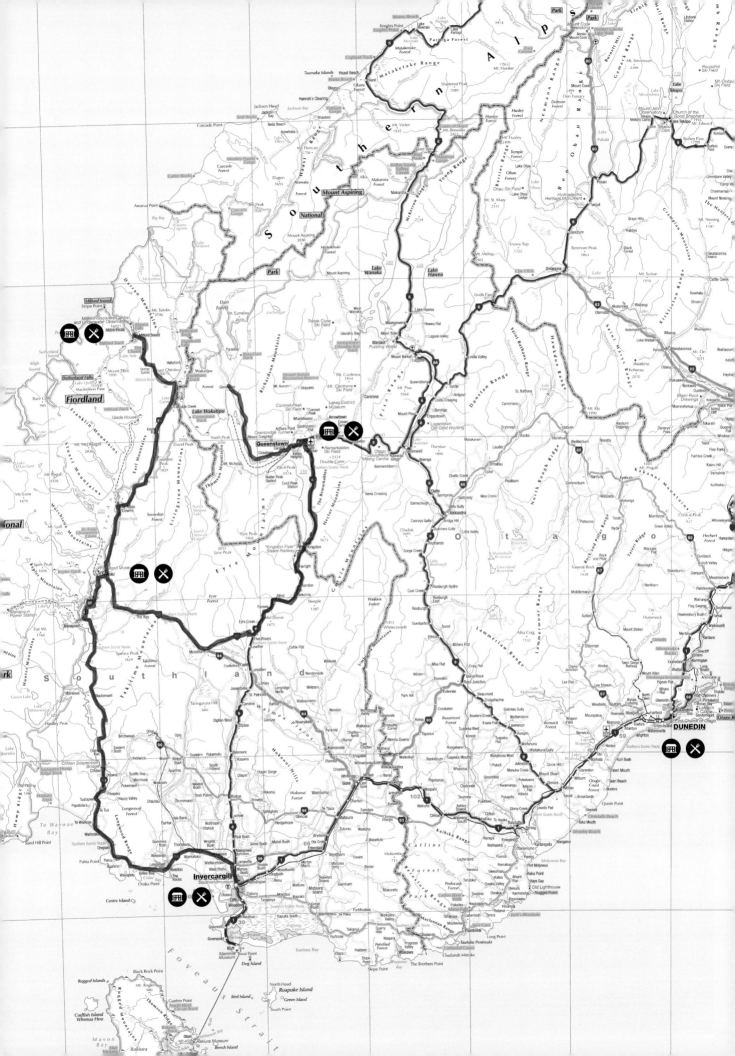

INVERCARGILL CHRISTCHURCH

1.086 KM • 3-4 TAGE // 675 MILES • 3-4 DAYS

Unterwegs hinter Invercargill. Das Land hält sich hier mit spektakulären Reizen zurück, da schweifen die Gedanken ab ... Ganz allgemein ist das Reisen in Neuseeland von großer Entspanntheit geprägt: Die Menschen sind außergewöhnlich herzlich und offen, der Verkehr dünn, die Straßen gut ausgebaut, das Klima freundlich.

—

We're on the move beyond Invercargill. The countryside here nothing special, so your thoughts start to wander... In general, traveling in New Zealand is a very relaxing experience: the people are exceptionally warm and friendly, the traffic is light, the roads are well built, the climate is pleasant.

DUNEDIN

Doch die Inseln am Ende der Welt haben durchaus auch ihre Schurken – eine Spezies, die sich dem sonnigen Flow unserer Reise zu allem entschlossen entgegenstellt. Wortwörtlich.

Trichosurus vulpecula, besser bekannt als „Possum" und nicht zu verwechseln mit dem Opossum, ist ein rund 30 bis 60 Zentimeter großes Beuteltier mit buschigem Schwanz, das aufgrund seines flauschigen Fells aus Australien exportiert und nach Neuseeland importiert wurde. Dieser vermeintliche Geniestreich jagdbeflissener Pelzliebhaber hat sich allerdings innerhalb eines starken Jahrhunderts zum Albtraum entwickelt, mittlerweile 70 Millionen Exemplare des fortpflanzungsfreudigen Tiers schädigen große Baumbestände empfindlich und bringen als Eier- und Kükenfresser einige der Vogelarten Neuseelands an den Rand des Aussterbens. Was also mit großen Kulleraugen und weichem Teddybärenfell unheimlich süß aussieht, ist mittlerweile zur meistgehassten Tierart Neuseelands geworden, deutlich vor den Kriebelmücken.

Glücklicherweise scheint sich Trichosurus vulpecula die eigene Unbeliebtheit sehr zu Herzen zu nehmen, denn das Possum wirft sich entlang mancher Straßen in eifrig-suizidärer Absicht vor jedes daherrollende Fahrzeug. Possum-Roadkill pflastert also ganze Streckenabschnitte – wobei natürlich nicht ausgeschlossen werden kann, dass der eine oder andere Neuseeländer bei Possum-Sichtung absichtlich Gas und Bremse verwechselt oder anstehende Ausweichmanöver nur eher halbherzig durchführt. Der in Neuseeland hingebungsvollen Possum-Abscheu haben wir uns trotzdem nicht anschließen wollen, gerade als Gast möchte man sich in diese internen Angelegenheiten der Einheimischen nur ungern einmischen. Weshalb wir das Angebot mancher Roadside-Dinners, einen herzhaften Possum-Eintopf zu genießen, auch aus der gebotenen Neutralität heraus diplomatisch abgelehnt haben. Der Vollständigkeit halber: Possum muss lange geschmort werden und soll nach einer Art fettigem Hase schmecken.

Die zähe Wartezeit fürs Garwerden eines herzhaften Possum-Stews investieren wir natürlich auch gerne produktiver – mit einigen Kilometern Fahrt von Invercargill bis zur Mündung des Mataura-Flusses bei Fortrose beispielsweise.

However, these islands at the end of the world also have their villains – a species that resolutely opposes every aspect of the sunny flow of our journey. Literally every aspect.

Trichosurus vulpecula, better known as the "possum" and not to be confused with the opossum, is a bushy-tailed marsupial measuring around 30 to 60 centimeters in size that was exported from Australia and imported to New Zealand for its soft fur. However, this supposed stroke of genius by hunting-mad fur lovers turned into a nightmare within a century. There are now 70 million of these fast-breeding animals, causing serious damage to large swathes of trees and, as greedy consumers of eggs and chicks, bringing some of New Zealand's bird species to the brink of extinction. What looks incredibly cute with big googly eyes and soft teddy bear fur has now become the most hated animal species in New Zealand, well ahead of midges.

Fortunately, Trichosurus vulpecula seems to be well aware of its own unpopularity. Possums throw themselves in front of every vehicle passing on some roads with eager, suicidal intent. Possum roadkill paves entire sections of the route – although it is possible that one or two New Zealanders will intentionally confuse the gas and brake pedals when they spot a possum, or will only half-heartedly execute evasive maneuvers. We were unwilling to join in with New Zealand's devoted hatred of possums – as guests you don't want to get involved in the internal affairs of the locals. It was in an effort to maintain the necessary neutrality that we diplomatically declined the offer in some roadside diners to enjoy a hearty possum stew. As a point of information: possum must be braised for a long time and is said to taste like a kind of fatty rabbit.

Naturally, we would prefer to invest the long time required waiting for a hearty possum stew in a more productive way – by driving a few kilometers from Invercargill to the mouth of the Mataura River near Fortrose, for example. The flat land down here has the same harsh uniformity as other coastal plains the world over, but beyond Fortrose things become hillier, more varied and more entertaining. The area around Porpoise Bay with the Waikawa River looks very impressive after so

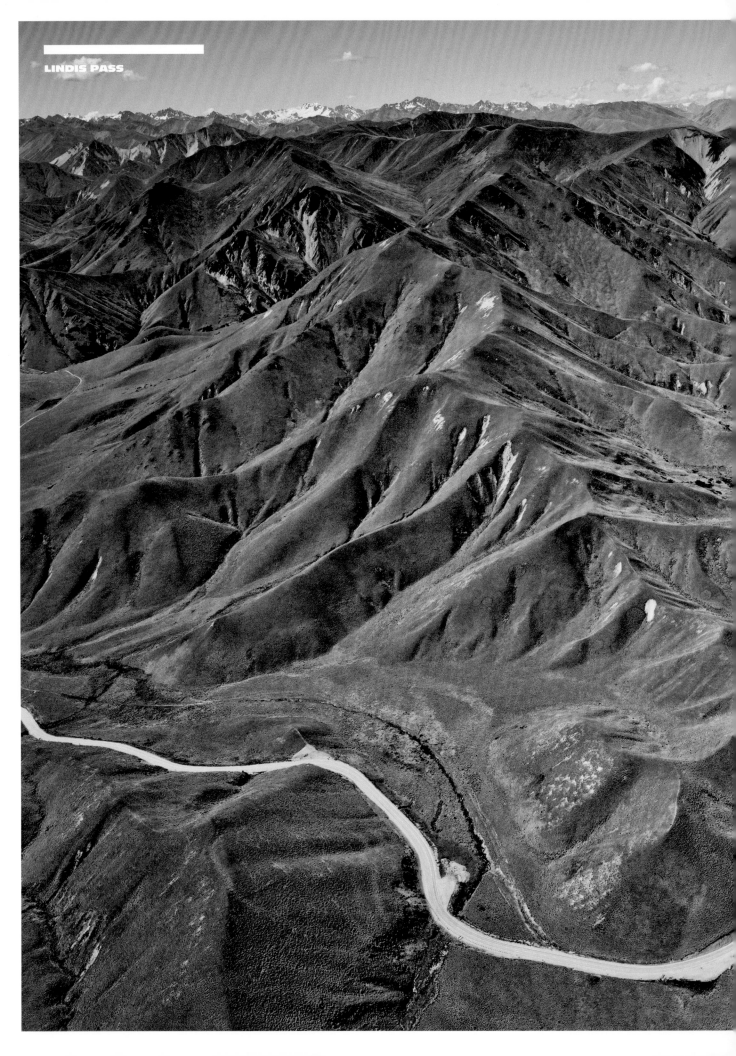

Das platte Land hier unten pflegt strecken-weise die herbe Gleichmäßigkeit anderer Küstenebenen auf dieser Welt, hinter Fort-rose wird es aber hügeliger, vielseitiger und unterhaltsamer. Die Gegend rund um die Porpoise Bay mit dem hier mündenden Waikawa-Fluss legt sich nach vielen Mei-len in landwirtschaftlich-gleichförmiger Umgebung ausgesprochen ins Zeug. Wer allerdings von den „Niagara Falls" ein paar hundert Meter weiter im Landesinneren dem Namen entsprechende Dramatik er-wartet, dürfte enttäuscht sein – es handelt sich hier um sanft strudelnde Stromschnel-len im Fluss. Ja, neuseeländischer Humor hat kein Problem damit, sich selbst auf die Schippe zu nehmen. Auch bei den kleinen Koropuku Falls, versteckt im Dickicht des wuchernden Catlins-Regenwalds, handelt es sich eher um eine Art XXL-Dusche. Die McLean Falls können da schon eher beein-drucken, indem sie rauschende Wasser-Kaskaden über mächtige Steinstufen schi-cken. Hinter der Brücke über den Tahako-pa-Fluss landen wir schließlich am dicht nebeneinander liegenden Duo aus den Matai- und Horseshoe-Wasserfällen, die unserer kleinen Ausfahrt in die Varianten-welt des Wasserfalls klassische Kalender-Motive hinzufügen: Felssturz im Wald, rauschende Gischt, Wasserbecken darun-ter. Wunderschön. Und jedes Mal den Spa-ziergang von der Straße wert.

Ruhig geht es weiter, aufmerksam für die Welt links und rechts der Straße. Über den Catlins River bis Owaka, dann zum Kaka Point an der Molyneux Bay und hinauf nach Balclutha: Heimliche Hauptstadt der Schafzüchter, Stadt am großen Clutha-Fluss, umgeben von sanft schwingendem, saftig grünem Hügelland. Noch einmal knapp 25 Kilometer weiter haben wir ei-nen Wendepunkt erreicht: Bei Milton wollten wir eigentlich wieder ins Landes-innere fahren, in Richtung Alexandra und Cromwell. Aber der Besuch in Dune-din, der Stadt am Otago Harbour muss doch noch sein: Wie ein enormer See zieht sich die Bucht vom Pazifik her hinter die Otago-Halbinsel und die Ecke dort oben ist

many miles of uniform agricultural sur-roundings. However, anyone expecting drama to match the name "Niagara Falls" a few hundred meters further inland will probably be disappointed – these are just gently swirling rapids in the river. You see, New Zealander have a sense of humor that has no problem making fun of itself. The small Koropuku Falls, hidden in the thicket of the overgrown Catlins rain-forest, are also more of a kind of oversized bathroom shower. The McLean Falls are more impressive, sending rushing water cascading over mighty stone steps. Be-yond the bridge over the Tahakopa River we finally end up at the shouder-to-shoul-der pairing of the Matai and Horseshoe waterfalls, which add classic calendar motifs to our little excursion into the di-verse world of the waterfall: rock falls in the forest, rushing spray, pools of water below. Beautiful. And worth the trek from the road every time.

We continue on in calm contemplation, alive to the world to our left and right on the road. We cross the Catlins River to Owa-ka, then push on to Kaka Point on Moly-neux Bay and up to Balclutha. Surround-ed by gently rolling, lush green hills, this town on the great Clutha River is the se-cret capital of sheep farming. Another 25 kilometers further on we reach a turning point: we originally intended to drive in-land again at Milton, heading for Alexan-dra and Cromwell.

Yet a visit to Dunedin, the city on the Otago Harbor, is still a must: the bay stretches from the Pacific beyond the Otago Penin-sula like an enormous lake and this cor-ner of the world should not be missed. Me-mories of driving across the Banks Penin-sula near Christchurch come flooding back – highlands on the Pacific, with picturesque hills and pockets of sea. You could spend days wandering through this beautiful area, hiking down to the little coves by the sea, sitting on the grass on wind-blown hilltops or feasting on seafood in the res-taurants of the harbor towns. Time stands

SCENIC FLIGHTS

TRUE SOUTH FLIGHTS LTD
1B/8 HAWTHORNE DRIVE
QUEENSTOWN
WWW.TRUESOUTHFLIGHTS.CO.NZ

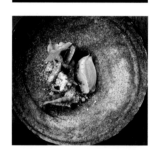

HOTEL & RESTAURANT

THE BATCH
173 SPEY STREET
INVERCARGILL

MOIETY
42 QUEENS GARDENS
CENTRAL DUNEDIN
WWW.MOIETY.RESTAURANT

FABLE DUNEDIN
310 PRINCES STREET
DUNEDIN
WWW.FABLEHOTELSANDRESORTS.COM

LINDIS PASS

LINDIS PASS

MOUNT COOK

einfach sehenswert. Erinnerungen an die Fahrt über die Banks-Halbinsel bei Christchurch steigen hoch – Highlands am Pazifik, mit pittoresken Hügeln und Meer im Inneren. Man könnte tagelang durch diese lieblichen Winkel streifen, hinunter zu den kleinen Buchten am Meer wandern, dann wieder auf windzerzausten Hügelkuppen im Gras sitzen oder Meeresfrüchte in den Restaurants der Hafenorte schlemmen.

HOTEL

THE HERMITAGE HOTEL MT COOK
89 TERRACE ROAD
MOUNT COOK VILLAGE
WWW.HERMITAGE.CO.NZ

LAKESTONE LODGE
4589 TEKAPO-TWIZEL RD
LAKE PUKAKI TWIZEL
WWW.LAKESTONELODGE.CO.NZ

Die Zeit steht still – wie lange, wissen wir nicht – und dann lösen wir uns wehmütig vom Otago Harbour. Rollen hinunter nach Milton und steigen endgültig in die letzte, große Reise unserer Fahrt durch Neuseeland ein. Weit, immer weiter, schwingt sich der Highway 8 im Rhythmus des Hügellands voran. Dreht bei Lawrence ein paar Grad nach Westen, korrigiert dann aber zurück auf fokussierten Nordwest-Kurs. Und nun trifft die Straße wieder einmal auf dieser Reise den Clutha-Fluss, scheint ganz erleichtert über dessen selbstbewusste Navigationshilfe zu sein und vertraut sich seiner Zielführung an. Durchs Goldgräberland. Durch immer rauer werdende Gegenden voller herber Berge und tiefer Schluchten, in denen man den ehemals frei dahinwandernden Strom in Stauseen sperrt. Der Clutha nimmt das stoisch hin, bewässert hinter Cromwell sogar hilfsbereit das Land und kurvt dann in vielen Windungen nach Westen, zum Lake Wanaka. Für uns würde sich dort ein Kreis schließen, wir würden unserer Route von der Westküste herüber begegnen und deshalb wünschen wir dem Clutha ein schönes Fluss-Leben, ziehen mit dem Highway 8 nach Norden, über den Lindis Pass.

Der ist unser Tor in die Alpen hinein, führt in weite Länder aus malerischer Einsamkeit, ein Reich aus Tälern und Hügelketten, schwingend, vibrierend in Erdtönen, in Farngrün, Strauchgrau, Moosrot, Felsschwarz und Kalkgelb. Und gerade wenn man glaubt, dass das alles nicht mehr majestätischer, hypnotischer, in sich gekehrter werden kann, landen wir hinter Twizel am Lake Pukaki.

still – although we don't know for how long – and then we regretfully leave Otago Harbor behind. We roll down to Milton and finally embark on the last big leg of our journey through New Zealand. Onward, ever onward, Highway 8 swings to the rhythm of the hill country. It turns a few degrees to the west at Lawrence, but then corrects itself, returning to a focused northwest course.

And now the road reencounters the Clutha River, seemingly relieved to have it as a confident navigation aid and trusting its route. We pass through gold rush country, through increasingly raw areas full of harsh mountains and deep gorges, where the previously free-flowing water is trapped in reservoirs. The Clutha accepts this imprisonment stoically, even helpfully irrigating the land beyond Cromwell and then following a twisting path westward, to Lake Wanaka. For us, this would mean coming full circle, meeting our route from the west coast and that's why we bid a fond farewell to the Clutha and head north on Highway 8, over the Lindis Pass.

This is our gateway to the Alps, leading into vast areas of picturesque solitude, a kingdom of valleys and hills, swinging, vibrating in earth tones: fern green, bush gray, moss red, rock black and lime yellow. And just when you think things can't get any more majestic, hypnotic and introspective, beyond Twizel we end up at Lake Pukaki, a seemingly enchanted, turquoise green hybrid creature of lake and sea. We follow the western shore, driving close to the north. Suddenly mountains appear behind the curves on the slopes that run down to the water, glistening white, mercilessly cold, devouring even the last warmth of all the sun's rays. The Aoraki massif or Mount Cook is the glacial head of the New Zealand Alps, the heart of the mountains. On the other side, these giants feed the Fox and Franz Josef glaciers. We find our minds wandering again to the scree rivers opening onto the Pacific.

Mit unbarmherziger Kälte selbst die letzte Wärme aller Sonnenstrahlen verschlingend. Das Massiv des Aoraki oder Mount Cook ist das gletscherbedeckte Haupt der neuseeländischen Alpen, das Herz der Berge. Auf der anderen Bergseite füttern diese Riesen den Fox- und Franz-Josef-Gletscher – in Gedanken streifen wir noch einmal dort drüben hinunter zu den Geröllflüssen am Pazifik.

Einem gefühlten Zwitterwesen aus See und Meer, türkisgrün und verzaubert, an dessen Westufer wir nah Norden fahren. So lange, bis hinter den Kurven in den zum Wasser abfallenden Hängen Berge auftauchen. Gleißend weiß. Mit unbarmherziger Kälte selbst die letzte Wärme aller Sonnenstrahlen verschlingend. Das Massiv des Aoraki oder Mount Cook ist das gletscherbedeckte Haupt der neuseeländischen Alpen, das Herz der Berge. Auf der anderen Bergseite füttern diese Riesen den Fox- und Franz-Josef-Gletscher – in Gedanken streifen wir noch einmal dort drüben hinunter zu den Geröllflüssen am Pazifik.

Eigentlich haben wir das Ende unserer Reise genau hier erreicht – am Fuß der Gipfel. Aber die Fahrt zurück in die Welt der Menschen dauert noch lange. Sie wird uns Stunden später, beim Hineinfahren in die Außenbezirke von Christchurch, geradezu vorkommen wie eine biblische Wanderung. Zurück ans Südufer des Lake Pukaki, nach Osten zum Lake Tekapo und dann Meile um Meile nach unten und nach Osten. In die weite Küstenebene rund um Christchurch hinaus. Erst dort enden wir. Bei den Menschen. Stellen unsere Fahrmaschine ab, stolpern mit steifen Beinen und langsam schlagendem Herzen in ein kleines Café. Dort warten wir geduldig, bis unsere Seele nachgekommen ist, von den Bergen herunter.

Suddenly mountains appear behind the curves on the slopes that run down to the water, glistening white, mercilessly cold, devouring even the last warmth of all the sun's rays. The Aoraki massif or Mount Cook is the glacial head of the New Zealand Alps, the heart of the mountains. On the other side, these giants feed the Fox and Franz Josef glaciers. We find our minds wandering again to the scree rivers opening onto the Pacific.

We have actually reached the end of our tour right here – at the foot of the peaks. But the journey back to the human world still takes a long time. Hours later, as we drive into the outskirts of Christchurch, it will seem almost like a biblical journey. We return to the south shore of Lake Pukaki, drive east to Lake Tekapo and then mile by mile downward and eastward.

We venture out into the vast coastal plain around Christchurch. Only there do we stop. Civilization. We park our car, stumble into a small café our legs stiff and our hearts beating slowly. There we wait patiently for our souls to come down from the mountains.

INVERCARGILL CHRISTCHURCH

Invercargill ist mit ihren rund 55.000 Einwohnern die südlichste Großstadt Neuseelands, hier starten wir in die letzte Etappe unserer Reise. Übrigens: Der südlichste Punkt Neuseelands liegt auf den rund 600 Kilometer entfernt im subantarktischen Ozean liegenden, unbewohnten Campbell-Inseln. Die Etappe hinter Invercargill beginnt mit vielen Kilometern in landwirtschaftlich geprägten Gegenden, groovt sich dann auf den Küstenstraßen südlich des Catlins National Forest ins Reisetempo ein und kurvt dann über Balclutha und Milton bis nach Dunedin. Die dort liegende Otago-Halbinsel ist diesen Abstecher auf jeden Fall wert. Zurück in Milton setzen wir die Fahrt in Richtung Nordwesten fort, gelangen im Landesinneren so bis Alexandra und fahren von hier in nördlicher Richtung bis zum Lake Pukaki. Der Pukaki-See ist ein Schmelzwasser-See der ehemaligen Gebirgsgletscher, an seinem Nordende thronen die schnee- und eisbedeckten Gipfel des Aoraki-/Mount-Cook-Massivs, die auch heute noch dicke Gletscherkappen bewahren. Wieder fahren wir den Weg zurück nach Süden, setzen dann die Reise am Südende des Sees weiter nach Osten, streifen den Lake Tekapo und rollen nun in Richtung Osten. Nach vielen Kilometern aus dem Gebirge hinaus und dann der Fahrt durch die vorgelagerte Küstenebene, sind wir wieder in Christchurch angelangt.

—

With a population of around 55,000, Invercargill is the southernmost city in New Zealand. This is where we start the last leg of our journey. By the way: the most southerly point of New Zealand is on the uninhabited Campbell Islands, around 600 kilometers away in the subantarctic ocean. The first part of the stage beyond Invercargill consists of many kilometers of agricultural land, after which we groove at cruising pace along the coastal roads south of the Catlins National Forest and then curve through Balclutha and Milton to Dunedin. The Otago Peninsula is definitely worth this detour. Back in Milton we continue our journey north-west, reaching Alexandra inland and from there driving north to Lake Pukaki. Lake Pukaki is a meltwater lake created by the former mountain glaciers; at its northern end are the snow- and ice-covered peaks of the Aoraki/Mount Cook massif, which still retain thick glacial caps today. We drive back south, then continue the journey east at the southern end of the lake, touch Lake Tekapo and now head east. After many kilometers we emerge from the mountains and then, after driving through the coastal plain, we arrive back in Christchurch.

1.086 KM • 3-4 TAGE // 675 MILES • 3-4 DAYS

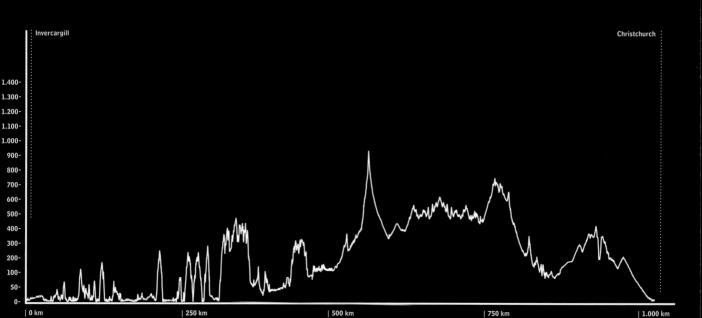

ASK THE LOCAL

>> *www.jeffreydocherty.com*

Er hat mehr als 20 Jahre Erfahrung in der Kreativbranche, unter anderem als Creative Director bei Nike, und gestaltete bereits Turnschuhe, Skateboards und Magazin-Cover. Seit seiner Kindheit faszinieren ihn aber auch Autos, vor allem luftgekühlte 911. Die Rede ist von Jeffrey Docherty, der mit seinen farbenfrohen Porsche-Kunstwerken auf Instagram seit einiger Zeit ein Millionenpublikum begeistert. Als gebürtiger Neusee-länder verbrachte er viele Jahre in Australien und in den USA und lebt jetzt wieder in seiner Heimat.

—

With more than 20 years of experience in the creative industry, as Creative Director at Nike, among others, he has designed sneakers, skateboards and magazine covers. But since his childhood he has also been fascinated by cars, especially by air-cooled 911s. Meet Jeffrey Docherty, whose colorful Porsche artwork on Instagram has been cap-tivating an audience of millions for some time now. Born in New Zealand, he spent many years in Australia and in the US and now lives back in his home country.

Erkläre unserem inneren Achtjährigen in drei Sätzen, was du machst. Ich erzähle Geschichten durch bewegte und statische Bilder.

Sind Autos Grafikdesign oder Produktdesign oder eher eine Produktion? Ich mag die persönliche Bindung, die wir zu Rennautos aufbauen. Sie beginnen als Produkte, sind aber durch die ikonischen Lackierungen, die uns in Erinnerung bleiben, sehr grafisch.

Wenn du Autodesigner wärst, welche Art von Auto würdest du intuitiv zuerst zeichnen? Für mich persönlich ist die Silhouette eines Coupés kaum zu übertreffen. Im Lauf der Jahrzehnte gab es so viele ikonische zweitürige Sportwagen. Vom 911 bis zum E-Type.

Die fünf heldenhaften Autos der Automobilgeschichte sind ...? Es scheint offensichtlich, aber der 911 RS 2.7 steht ganz oben auf der Liste, dicht gefolgt von einem 356 mit bent- oder split-window. Mk1 Mini Cooper S, Subaru 22B, und ein Mk2 GT40.

Wenn du von nun an nur noch Autos in einer Farbe fahren könntest, welche wäre das? Mir gefällt der zeitlose und mutige Look schwarzer Autos. Außerdem bringen sie die Designlinien so gut zur Geltung.

Welches Auto fährst du zurzeit und warum? Ich habe im Moment ein paar Oldtimer, aber ich fühle mich besonders zu meinem Mk1 Mini Cooper S hingezogen. Es macht so viel Spaß, damit zu fahren, dass ich immer mit einem Lächeln nach Hause komme, wenn ich mit ihm unterwegs war. Ich habe ihn kurz nach meiner Rückkehr aus den USA nach Neuseeland gekauft, und ich erinnere mich gern daran, wie ich als junger Mann in einem solchen Auto fahren gelernt habe.

Wenn Besucher in Neuseeland nur eine Route fahren dürften, wo würdest du sie hinschicken? Ich habe das Glück, in der Nähe einiger großartiger Straßen auf der Banks Peninsula auf der Südinsel zu leben. Die Fahrt nach Akaroa ist kurz, aber landschaftlich sehr reizvoll, und man kann unterwegs in Little River auf einen Kaffee anhalten. Die Kurven und die Aussicht auf die Bucht sind großartig.

Warum sollte jeder mindestens einmal nach Neuseeland reisen? Ich glaube, es ist noch ziemlich ursprünglich, nicht überbevölkert und verbaut. Dadurch, dass es so abgelegen und isoliert ist, wirkt es so entspannt.

Wo ist deiner Meinung nach der schönste Ort Neuseelands? Die Abel-Tasman-Region ist magisch. Die goldenen Strände, das klare blaue Wasser und die üppigen grünen Landschaften sind optisch sehr ansprechend.

Explain to our inner eight-year-old what you do in three sentences. I tell stories through moving and static pictures.

Are cars graphic design or product design or more of a production? I love how we form personal attachments with race cars. They start life as products but are very graphic in nature with the iconic liveries that stick with us.

If you were a car designer, what kind of car would you intuitively draw first? Personally, I find the silhouette of a coupé hard to beat. Through the decades so many iconic cars have all been two-door sports cars, from the 911 to the E-Type.

The five hero cars in automotive history are...? It seems obvious but the 911 RS 2.7 is top of the list, closely followed by a 356 Bent or Split Window. Mk1 Mini Cooper S, Subaru 22B, and a Mk2 GT40.

If you could only drive cars in one color from now on, what would it be? I love the timeless and bold look of black cars. They also show the design lines so well.

What car are you currently driving and why? I have a few classic cars right now, but I seem to be gravitating to my Mk1 Mini Cooper S. It is so fun to drive, I always return home with a smile after I've been out driving in it. I bought it recently after returning to New Zealand from the US, I have lots of fond memories learning to drive in one as a young lad.

If visitors to New Zealand could only travel one route, where would you send them? I am lucky to live near some great drives on the Banks Peninsula in the South Island. It is a short drive to Akaroa but a very scenic one and you can stop in Little River along the way for a coffee. The curves and bay views are great.

Why should everyone visit New Zealand at least once? I think it is still pretty well preserved, not overpopulated

**Was sind deine Lieblingsstrecken außerhalb Neusee-
lands?** Ich liebe den Pacific Coast Highway, die kalifor-
nische Küste und Oregon. Eigentlich jeden Ort an der
Westküste mit Blick auf den Ozean und kurvenreichen
Straßen. Als ich in Oregon lebte, war es nur eine kurze
Fahrt zur Küste, also habe ich dort viel Zeit verbracht.

Elektroantrieb oder Verbrennungsmotor? Beides. Ich
finde es toll, was die LMP1- oder Le-Mans-Prototypen an
Leistung und Möglichkeiten bieten. Wobei es schwer ist,
den Klang eines Sechszylinder-Boxers bei hohen Dreh-
zahlen zu übertreffen.

**Wo hattest du den besten/schrecklichsten Moment
auf der Straße und warum?** Ich hatte meinen 911 gerade nach einer zweijährigen Restaurierung aus der Werk-
statt geholt. Mit ein paar Freunden fuhr ich in die Berge
bei Portland, Oregon. Leider hatte ich vergessen, meine
Fronthaube zu verriegeln. Also flog die Glasfaserhaube
hoch und klappte über Dach und Windschutzscheibe, als
ich mit hoher Geschwindigkeit durch einen Tunnel fuhr.
Kein schöner Moment – null Sicht. Zum Glück gelang es
mir, sicher anzuhalten.

**Mit welchem berühmten Beifahrer würdest du gern
einmal verreisen?** In letzter Zeit verfolge ich die Formel 1
sehr intensiv. Mit einigen der Piloten würde ich gern fahren und mit ihnen plaudern, um einen Insider-Bericht
der Formel 1 und ihren Lebensstil zu bekommen. Lando
Norris oder Lewis Hamilton. Ich bin sicher, die hätten ein
paar Geschichten zu erzählen.

Und was läuft in deinem Autoradio? Das klingt vielleicht
seltsam, aber ich habe in keinem meiner Autos ein funk-
tionierendes Radio. Das liegt vor allem daran, dass es sich
um Oldtimer handelt. Ich bin aber ein großer Verfechter
von purem Motorengeräusch und konzentriere mich auf
das Fahrerlebnis.

and developed. The fact that it is so remote and isolated
helps to keep it feeling relaxed.

**Where do you think the most beautiful place in New
Zealand is?** The Abel Tasman region is magic. The golden
beaches, clear blue water, and lush green landscapes make
it very visually appealing.

What are your favorite routes outside of New Zealand?
I love the Pacific Coast Highway, Coastal California, and
Oregon. Anywhere with ocean views and winding roads
along the West Coast. When I lived in Oregon it was a
quick trip to the coastline, so I spent a bit of time there.

Electric drive or combustion engine? Both. I love what
the LMP1 or Prototype Le Mans cars are doing in terms of
performance and capabilities. That said, it is hard to beat
the sound of a high-revving flat 6.

**Where did you have the best/horrible moment on the
road and why?** I had just got my 911 back from the shop
after a two-year restoration. After meeting up with some
friends we took off up into the hills near Portland, Oregon.
Unfortunately, I forgot to latch my hood straps and my fi-
berglass hood flew up and folded over the roof/window as
I ripped through a tunnel at speed. Not a fun moment – zero
visibility. Luckily, I managed to stop safely.

**Which famous passenger would you really like to go on a
trip with?** I've been following the F1 a lot lately, so I'd love
to drive and chat with some of the drivers to get an insider's
take on F1 and the lifestyle they live. Lando Norris or Lewis
Hamilton. I'm sure they'd have a few stories worth telling.

And what's on your car radio? This might sound strange,
but I don't actually have a working radio in any of my
cars. Mostly because they are all classics. I am a big advo-
cate for pure engine sounds and focusing on the driving
experience.

WORTH A VISIT: BILL RICHARDSON TRANSPORT WORLD

BILL RICHARDSON TRANSPORT WORLD
491 TAY STREET, HAWTHORNDALE
INVERCARGILL
WWW.TRANSPORTWORLD.CO.NZ

Und dann wäre da ja noch das große, weiße Gebäude mit den roten Streifen zwischen dem Stadtzentrum von Invercargill und dem Ascot Park Raceway. An der Ausfallstraße nach Osten steht es, sieht mit den abgerundeten Ecktürmen zum State Highway 1 hin und den großen Art-Deco-Schriftzügen aus wie eine Vintage-Jukebox. Die perfekte Verpackung für einen Ort voller motorisiert-nostalgischer Geheimnisse. Und die „Bill Richardson Transport World" ist genau das: eine Schatztruhe, gefüllt mit der Magie vergangener Jahrzehnte.

Über Jahrzehnte hinweg hat der Transport-Unternehmer Bill Richardson in Invercargill alte Lastkraftwagen und anderes Maschinen-Material der handfesteren Sorte zusammengetragen und aufwendig restauriert. Die stetig wachsende Sammlung sollte dabei aber keinesfalls nur eine persönliche Liebelei sein, sondern wurde immer wieder einer begeisterten Öffentlichkeit zugänglich gemacht. Als Bill Richardson 2005 überraschend starb, wusste seine Familie was sein letzter Wille in Bezug auf die über 300 Ausstellungsexemplare umfassende Sammlung war: Sie sollte weiterhin Menschen Freude machen. Zehn Jahre nach seinem Tod eröffnete die „Bill Richardson Transport World" in Invercargill als intensives 360-Grad-Erlebnis. Die Familie Richardson hat sich des väterlichen Erbes angenommen und eigene Interessen und Ideen eingebracht. Im Eingangsbereich lockt das „Grille Café" mit Soulfood, in den Ausstellungen werden die makellos restaurierten Trucks von einer umfangreichen Sammlung klassischer Autos komplimentiert. Selbst beim Toilettengang gibt es Witziges, Kurioses, Spannendes aus früheren Jahrzehnten zu entdecken.

Wir bei CURVES haben hier großartige, vergnügte Stunden verbracht, gestaunt und gelacht, jede Menge sentimentale Erinnerungstränen verdrückt. Danke, Bill Richardson!

We contemplate the big white building with red stripes located between Invercargill city center and Ascot Park Raceway. It stands on the arterial road to the east and looks like a vintage jukebox with its art deco lettering and its rounded corner towers facing onto State Highway 1. The exterior couldn't be more perfect for a place packed with motorized, nostalgic secrets. "Bill Richardson Transport World" is exactly that: a treasure chest filled with the magic of past decades.

For decades, transport entrepreneur Bill Richardson in Invercargill has collected and painstakingly restored old trucks and other heavy-weight transport machinery. This ever-growing collection was never intended as just a personal affair, but was made continuously available to an enthusiastic public almost from the start. When Bill Richardson died unexpectedly in 2005, his family knew what his final wish would have been for the collection, which included over 300 exhibits: it should continue to bring joy to people.

Ten years after his death, "Bill Richardson Transport World" opened in Invercargill as an intensive, immersive experience. The Richardson family has built on their father's legacy, incorporating their own interests and ideas. The "Grille Café" in the entrance area serves delicious soul food and the immaculately restored trucks are no longer the only show in town, but are complemented by an extensive collection of classic cars. Even when you use the rest-rooms you can discover funny, curious and exciting things from previous decades.

We at CURVES spent a great, happy time here, marveling and laughing and shedding lots of sentimental tears of remembrance. Thank you, Bill Richardson!

BAC KST AGE

Feste drücken, Koffer zu. „Tschüss", sagen wir mit vor Vorfreude strahlenden Augen, „auf nach Neuseeland!" – Die Kids aus dem erweiterten CURVES-Universum sind es gewohnt, dass wir immer wieder mal das Weite suchen, aber Neuseeland, das interessiert sie wirklich: „Wo ist das eigentlich," fragen sie, „wo liegt Neuseeland denn?" – Und weil alle guten Antworten so sind, dass selbst Kinder sie verstehen, holen wir tief Luft und erzählen was vom anderen Ende der Welt. Unten auf der Erdkugel. Und damit gehen die Fragen erst richtig los: Wie lang der Tunnel eigentlich sein müsste, um sich nach Neuseeland durchzubohren. Was eigentlich passiert, wenn man aus Versehen daneben bohrt und den Ozean trifft, ob dann der ganze Pazifik durch den Tunnel auf unserer Seite herausläuft. Ob Wasser in Neuseeland tatsächlich andersherum aus einer Badewanne läuft als auf der Nordhalbkugel. Ob Winter in Neuseeland wirklich Sommer ist und Sommer Winter. Ob es auf Neuseeland Drachen gibt. Ob dort Menschenfresser wohnen. Ob es Neuseeland wirklich gibt oder nur ausgedacht ist, weil der Name „Neuseeland" klingt wie aus einem Kinderbuch.

Weshalb die Leute dort auf der anderen Seite nicht von der Erdkugel herunterfallen ... Und während wir geduldig eine Frage nach der anderen so gründlich es nur geht beantworten, denken wir, dass das verdammt gute Fragen sind. Dass wir sie uns insgeheim auch alle schon irgendwann einmal gestellt haben. Plus irgendwas mit

Press down hard to close your suitcase. "Bye now," we say, our eyes shining with anticipation. "We're off to New Zealand!" – The kids from the extended CURVES family are used to these goodbyes, but New Zealand is what really interests them: "Where is that actually," they ask. "Where is New Zealand?" – Because all the good answers are simple enough so that even children can understand them, we take a deep breath and tell them a little about the other end of the world. Down on the other side of the globe. And that's when the questions really start: How long would the tunnel actually have to be to dig through to New Zealand? What actually happens if you missed the land and accidentally hit the ocean? Would the entire Pacific drain through the tunnel to our side. Does the water actually flow out of a bathtub in New Zealand the opposite way to the northern hemisphere? Is it true that winter is really summer in New Zealand and summer is winter? Are there dragons in New Zealand?

What about cannibals? Does New Zealand really exist or is it just made up because the name "New Zealand" sounds like something out of a children's book? Why don't the people on the other side of the world simply fall off? As we patiently answer this cross-examination as thoroughly as we can, we think these are damn good questions. We have all secretly faced them at some point. Plus something about sheep, tattooed men sticking their tongues out at each other... and hobbits. It's an incredibly

Schafen, mit tätowierten Männern, die sich gegenseitig die Zunge herausstrecken, und mit Hobbits. Aus dem CURVES-Zuhause im Süden Deutschlands ist es ein unfassbar weiter Weg rund um den Globus, man hat also eine Menge Zeit, sich all die spannenden Fragen durch den Kopf gehen zu lassen. Und wenn man dann irgendwann das Innere eines Flugzeugs nicht mehr sehen mag, ist man angekommen. Völlig unwirklich. In Neuseeland. Und fühlt sich tatsächlich ein wenig auf dem Kopf stehend. Bei zwölf Stunden Zeitunterschied wird man eben zur reisenden Wendejacke – das Innerste nach außen gedreht und das Äußere nach innen.

Eine Reise durch Neuseeland startet man also in gegenläufigem Biorhythmus, lässt sich Zeit, legt im Autoradio Cole Porter ein: „Night and day, you are the one, only you beneath the moon and under the sun. Whether near to me or far, it's no matter darling where you are, I think of you, night and day." – Das hilft. Und die Tatsache, dass Neuseeland für Europäer gar nicht so fremd scheint, wie es die unfassbare Entfernung vermuten lassen könnte. Die Landschaften sprechen keinen exotischen Dialekt, sie erzählen keine fremdartigen Geschichten. Immer wieder erinnert uns das Land an die europäischen Alpen, an Skandinavien oder Schottland, an den Süden Frankreichs oder den ligurischen Nordwesten Italiens. Es ist eine unter der Oberfläche liegende Stimmung, die Neuseeland so besonders macht, die in Flora und Fauna spürbare Anderweltigkeit einer evolutionären Entwicklung abseits des Rests der Welt: Ins bekannte Bild der Gräser, Blüten, Bäume und Sträucher mischen sich Pflanzen, die es so nur in Neuseeland gibt, und werden hier zu einer Farbe, die alles ändert. Und dann ist da in manchen Momenten eine eigentümliche Dramatik oder sehnsüchtig an Herzen ziehende Schönheit, die das Land zwischen Pazifik und Antarktis auszeichnet. Berge, majestätischer als bekannte Berge. Schnee, gleißender als anderer Schnee. Flüsse, reißender als wilde Wasser anderswo. Sanftheit im Kleinen, lieblicher als wir es von bisherigen Reisen kennen. Selbst in den einsamsten Winkeln, den höchsten Höhen bleibt Neuseeland ein freundliches und offenes Land.

All diese Elemente haben wir auf unserer Fahrt durch Neuseeland auch durch die Menschen erlebt: Auf kaum einer anderen Reise wurden wir so gelassen und warmherzig interessiert empfangen, die Neuseeländer pflegen einen entwaffnend angenehmen Umgang mit Fremden. Die Kultur ist eindeutig angelsächsisch eingefärbt, oft werfen die Ortschaften und Namen und sogar die Küche das milde Spiegelbild einer noch nicht restlos abgeschlossenen Vergangenheit Neuseelands als Teil des britischen Empires. Allerdings machen sich auch die alten Einflüsse Frankreichs und andauernden Einflüsse Asiens ebenso bemerkbar wie die tiefenentspannte Coolness eines Landes am Ende der Welt. In Neuseeland wirkt das Tempo des immer schneller drehenden Erdballs tatsächlich angenehm weit entfernt. Man wechselt mit dem Flug nach Auckland oder Christchurch in ein überschaubares Paralleluniversum, in dem das

long way around the globe from the CURVES home territory in southern Germany, so you have a lot of time to think about all these exciting questions. At some point, when you no longer want to see the inside of an airplane, you find you have arrived. It is completely unreal. You're in New Zealand. Things really do feel a little upside down. The twelve-hour time difference turns you into a traveling reversible jacket – the inside turned outwards and the outside turned inwards.

You start your trip around New Zealand in opposite biorhythms, taking your time and listening to Cole Porter on the car radio: "Night and day, you are the one, only you beneath the moon and under the sun. Whether near to me or far, it's no matter darling where you are, I think of you, night and day." – That helps. That and the fact that New Zealand doesn't seem as foreign to Europeans as its incredible distance might suggest. The landscapes do not speak any exotic dialect or tell any strange stories. The country repeatedly reminds us of the European Alps, Scandinavia or Scotland, the south of France or Liguria in northwest Italy. It is the atmosphere that lies beneath the surface that makes New Zealand so special, the otherworldliness of an evolutionary path that diverged from the rest of the world that can be witnessed in the flora and fauna: mixed into the familiar picture of grasses, flowers, trees and bushes are plants that are only native to New Zealand, and here they take on a color that changes everything. And then at some moments there is a strange drama or a longing, heart-tugging beauty that characterizes the country between the Pacific and Antarctica. The mountains are more majestic than our own more familiar mountains. The snow glitters brighter than other snow. River rapids rage more than the white water found elsewhere. We encounter gentleness on a small scale, sweeter than anything we have known from previous trips. Even in the loneliest corners and at the highest altitudes, New Zealand remains a friendly and open country.

We also experienced all of these elements through the people we met on our trip through New Zealand: on hardly any other trip have we been received with such calm and warm interest; the New Zealanders have a disarmingly pleasant way with strangers. The culture is clearly Anglo-Saxon in color, the towns and names and even the cuisine often mildly reflect the fact that New Zealand has not yet fully left behind its past as part of the British Empire. However, the old influences of France and the ongoing influences of Asia are also noticeable, as is the deeply relaxed coolness of a country at the end of the world. In New Zealand, the pace of the ever-faster rotating globe actually seems pleasantly distant. When you fly to Auckland or Christchurch, you switch to a manageable parallel universe in which the noise of global upheaval seems less intimidating and unsettling than elsewhere. Auckland? Christchurch? – Good keywords. On our trip through New

Knirschen globaler Verwerfungen weniger einschüchternd und beunruhigend wirkt als anderswo. Auckland? Christchurch? – Gute Stichworte. Bei unserer Reise durch Neuseeland haben wir uns ausschließlich auf die dünner besiedelte Südinsel konzentriert. Das ist ganz bestimmt keine gelebte Ignoranz gegenüber den Schönheiten und Sehenswürdigkeiten der Nordinsel mit ihren Großstädten Auckland und Wellington, sondern liegt einfach daran, dass wir uns mit CURVES auf die Suche nach einem ganz bestimmten Reiseziel machen: dem Unterwegssein auf den besten, schönsten, spektakulärsten, mitreißendsten Straßen des Planeten. Und die finden wir in absoluter Zuverlässigkeit dort, wo es nicht allzu viele Menschen gibt. Dass über 80 Prozent der Neuseeländer in den großen Städten leben und die auf der flächenmäßig kleineren Nordinsel liegen, bedeutet im Umkehrschluss, dass die epischen Straßen Neuseelands auf der nur dünn besiedelten Südinsel zu finden sind. Erstens. Und zweitens wird die Südinsel vom viele Hunderte Kilometer langen Gebirgszug der neuseeländischen Alpen geprägt. Was an Kurvensucher wie uns eine ähnliche Botschaft sendet, wie die Eichenwälder des Piemont an Trüffelhunde: Fahrfreudeintensive Straßen voraus!

Dass wir nach der Heimkehr von dieser Suche uneingeschränkten Erfolg vermelden können, liegt auch an einem ganz besonderen Reisegenossen, den wir von Porsche Neuseeland zur Verfügung gestellt bekommen haben: Der Porsche 911 T passte zu den weiten Reiseetappen im „Land der langen, weißen Wolke" ebenso perfekt wie zu den Serpentinen der Berge und den Kurven am Ozean. Als gehaltvolle Essenz des ikonischen Porsche-Sportwagens ist der 911 T eine langsam unter die Haut gehende Roadtripping-Legende. Kein überdrehter Aufreger, kein Selbstdarsteller, der die Schönheit von Reise und Landschaft übertönt, sondern ein souveräner Auto-Kumpel, mit dem das Erlebnis der Reise in all ihren Facetten intensiver und stärker und echter wird. Wir haben ihn ins Herz geschlossen, uns beim Abschied noch einmal lange nach ihm umgedreht. Danke, Porsche, für die Möglichkeit diese Freundschaft zu schließen. Danke auch an all die anderen Mitreisenden, die aus der Ferne oder konkret vor Ort dabei waren. Mit Unterstützung und guten Tipps, Freundlichkeit und Begeisterung. CURVES ist nicht die Reise eines Einzelnen, sondern die Reise von Gefährten. Ihr wisst, wer ihr seid. Danke schön.

Ihr macht möglich, dass die Reise immer weitergeht. Und jetzt sitzen wir vor Festplatten voller Bilder und Film-Material. Festgehaltene Momente, die sich im Laufe von 30 Tagen in Neuseeland, auf über 6.400 Fahrkilometern sowie unzähligen Drohnen-, Helikopter- und Cessna-Flugmeilen angesammelt haben. Dass die CURVES-Community nach über einem Jahrzehnt immer noch mit auf Reise geht und sogar größer wird, ist ein Privileg. Manchmal denken wir, dass die eigentliche Reise das Fotografieren, Filmen und Schreiben ist. Das Erzählen von den Flow-Momenten auf diesem herrlichen Planeten. Danke, dass Ihr dabei seid. Wir sehen uns.

Zealand we focused exclusively on the sparsely populated South Island. This is definitely not born of a decision to ignore the beauties and sights of the North Island with its major cities Auckland and Wellington, but is simply because with CURVES we are looking for a very specific travel destination: traveling to the best, most beautiful, most spectacular, most thrilling roads on the planet. We know with absolute certainty that these are found in places where there aren't too many people. The fact that over 80 percent of New Zealanders live in the big cities and are located on the smaller North Island means that the epic roads of New Zealand can be found on the sparsely populated South Island. That's the first thing. The second thing is that the South Island is shaped by the New Zealand Alps mountain range, which is hundreds of kilometers long. This is a signal to curve seekers like us rather like the one the oak forests of Piedmont emit to truffle dogs: the road ahead will be packed with intense driving pleasure!

The fact that we can report unqualified success after returning home from this trip is also due to a very special travel companion that Porsche New Zealand supplied: the Porsche 911 T was the ideal traveling companion for the long journey stages in the "land of the long, white cloud". just as perfect as the twists of the mountains and the curves of the ocean. The essential iconic Porsche sports car, the 911 T is a road trip legend that slowly gets under your skin. This is not the car for over-the-top excitement. It is not a self-promoter that drowns out the beauty of the journey and landscape, but a confident automotive factotum that makes every facet of the journey more intense, stronger and more real. We took it to our hearts and spent a long time saying our goodbyes. Thank you, Porsche, for the opportunity to forge this friendship.

Thanks also to all the other people who were part of our journey, whether from afar or on the ground. They provided invaluable support and great tips, as well as kindness and enthusiasm. CURVES is not a journey by one individual, but requires companions. You know who you are. Thank you all so much. You make it possible for these trips to happen.

And now we're faced with hard drives full of pictures and film material. Special moments captured over the course of 30 days in New Zealand, over 6,400 kilometers of driving and countless drone, helicopter and Cessna flight miles. The fact that the CURVES community is still traveling with us after more than a decade and continues to grow is a true privilege. Sometimes we think that the real journey happens in the photography, filming and writing, in other words when telling the story of the flow moments on this beautiful planet. Thank you for joining us. See you soon.

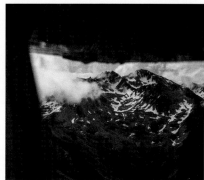

DANK AN / THANKS TO

Caitlin Ryan, Greg Clarke, Mark Milligan, April Huang, Yannick Ott, David Steca, Matthias Wagner, Frank Thiele, Hanno Vienken, Michael Dorn, Fabian Isensee, Michaela Bogner

SPECIAL FX / SPECIAL FX

Porsche New Zealand & Porsche Asia Pacific, Truesouthflights, AOT Travel - Christian Preiherr,

CURVES TRAVEL AGENT:

AOT Travel • info@aottravel.de • Tel. +49 89 12 24 800

ROUTE AS GPX FILE:

Porsche 992 T

911 Carrera T: Kraftstoffverbrauch* kombiniert (WLTP) 10,9 – 10,3 l/100 km, CO_2 Emissionen* kombiniert (WLTP) 247 – 233 g/km
911 Carrera T: Fuel consumption* combined (WLTP) 10.9 – 10.3 l/100 km, CO_2 emissions* combined (WLTP) 247 – 233 g/km

IMPRESSUM / IMPRINT

HERAUSGEBER/
PUBLISHER: CURVES MAGAZIN
THIERSCHSTRASSE 25
D-80538 MÜNCHEN

VERANTWORTLICH FÜR
DEN HERAUSGEBER/
RESPONSIBLE FOR
PUBLICATION:
STEFAN BOGNER

KONZEPT/CONCEPT:
STEFAN BOGNER
THIERSCHSTRASSE 25
D-80538 MÜNCHEN
SB@CURVES-MAGAZIN.COM

DELIUS KLASING
CORPORATE PUBLISHING
SIEKERWALL 21
D-33602 BIELEFELD

REDAKTION/
EDITORIAL CONTENT:
STEFAN BOGNER
BEN WINTER

ART DIRECTION, LAYOUT,
FOTOS/ART DIRECTION,
LAYOUT, PHOTOS:
STEFAN BOGNER

MAKING OF PHOTOS:
FRANK THIELE

TEXT/TEXT: BEN WINTER
TEXT INTRO/TEXT INTRO:
BEN WINTER

MOTIVAUSARBEITUNG,
LITHOGRAPHIE, SATZ/

POST-PRODUCTION,
LITHOGRAPHY, SETTING:
MICHAEL DORN

KARTENMATERIAL/MAP
MATERIAL: MAIRDUMONT,
OSTFILDERN

ÜBERSETZUNG/TRANSLATION:
JAMES O'NEILL

PRODUKTIONSLEITUNG/
PRODUCTION MANAGEMENT:
AXEL GERBER

DRUCK/PRINT:
KUNST- UND WERBEDRUCK,
BAD OEYNHAUSEN

1. AUFLAGE/1ST EDITION:
ISBN: 978-3-667-12843-0

AUSGEZEICHNET MIT / AWARDED WITH

DDC GOLD - DEUTSCHER DESIGNER CLUB E.V. FÜR GUTE GESTALTUNG 2011 // IF COMMUNICATION DESIGN AWARD 2012
BEST OF CORPORATE PUBLISHING 2012 // ADC BRONZE 2011 // RED DOT BEST OF THE BEST & D&AD 2012 // NOMINIERT
FÜR DEN DEUTSCHEN DESIGNPREIS 2015 // WINNER AUTOMOTIVE BRAND CONTEST 2016 // GOOD DESIGN AWARD 2014

CURVES AUSGABEN / OTHER ISSUES OF CURVES

PYRENÄEN
PYRENEES
Im Handel erhältlich/Available in stores

ÖSTERREICH
AUSTRIA
Im Handel erhältlich/Available in stores

SCHWEIZ
SWITZERLAND
Im Handel erhältlich/Available in stores

SCHOTTLAND
SCOTLAND
Im Handel erhältlich/Available in stores

FRANKREICH
FRANCE
Im Handel erhältlich/Available in stores

USA · KALIFORNIEN
USA · CALIFORNIA
Im Handel erhältlich/Available in stores

SIZILIEN
SICILY
Im Handel erhältlich/Available in stores

NORDITALIEN
NORTHERN ITALY
Im Handel erhältlich/Available in stores

OSTDEUTSCHLAND
EASTERN GERMANY
Im Handel erhältlich/Available in stores

DEUTSCHLAND/DÄNE.
GERMANY/DENMARK
Im Handel erhältlich/Available in stores

SPANIEN · MALLORCA
SPAIN · MALLORCA
Im Handel erhältlich/Available in stores

USA · COLORADO/UTAH
USA · COLORADO/UTAH
Im Handel erhältlich/Available in stores

THAILAND
THAILAND
Im Handel erhältlich/Available in stores

SÜDDEUTSCHLAND
SOUTHERN GERMANY
Im Handel erhältlich/Available in stores

PORTUGAL
PORTUGAL
Im Handel erhältlich/Available in stores

ISLAND
ICELAND
Im Handel erhältlich/Available in stores

MALAYSIA
MALAYSIA
Im Handel erhältlich/Available in stores

NORWEGEN
NORWAY
Im Handel erhältlich/Available in stores

PATAGONIEN
PATAGONIA
Im Handel erhältlich/Available in stores

KORSIKA
CORSICA
Im Handel erhältlich/Available in stores

Take your sports car fascination beyond the open road.

ELEVATE YOUR STYLE WITH THE
PORSCHE LIFESTYLE COLLECTION.

PORSCHE